C000133615

Making Progress

to First Certificate

Student's Book

Leo Jones

CAMBRIDGE
UNIVERSITY PRESS

PUBLISHED BY THE PRESS SYNDICATE OF THE UNIVERSITY OF CAMBRIDGE
The Pitt Building, Trumpington Street, Cambridge, United Kingdom

CAMBRIDGE UNIVERSITY PRESS
The Edinburgh Building, Cambridge CB2 2RU, UK
40 West 20th Street, New York, NY 10011–4211, USA
477 Williamstown Road, Port Melbourne, VIC 3207, Australia
Ruiz de Alarcón 13, 28014 Madrid, Spain
Dock House, The Waterfront, Cape Town 8001, South Africa

http://www.cambridge.org

© Cambridge University Press 2005

This book is in copyright. Subject to statutory exception
and to the provisions of relevant collective licensing agreements,
no reproduction of any part may take place without
the written permission of Cambridge University Press.

First published 2005
Printed in the United Kingdom at the University Press, Cambridge

Text typefaces Minion and Meta Plus Medium, System QuarkXpress® [HAR]

A catalogue record for this book is available from The British Library

ISBN 0 521 53702 9 Student's Book
ISBN 0 521 53703 7 Self-Study Student's Book
ISBN 0 521 53704 5 Teacher's Book
ISBN 0 521 53705 3 Workbook
ISBN 0 521 53706 1 Workbook with Answers
ISBN 0 521 53707 X Set of 2 audio cassettes
ISBN 0 521 53708 8 Set of 2 audio CDs

Cover design by Andrew Oliver
Produced by Hardlines Limited, Charlbury

Contents

Thanks

A big thank you to everyone who helped to create this course!

Thanks to the teachers who commented on work in progress and suggested many improvements:

Christine Barton, Greece; Annette Brechbuhl, Switzerland; Henny Burke, Spain; Hugh Cory, Italy; Alex Case, Japan; Konstantina Diroplaki, Greece; Nicole Gaudet, Germany; Alexander Hall, Germany; Kirsten Holt, UK; Miranda Karjagdiu, Turkey; Hayley Maxwell, UK; Mitzi Powles, Italy; Rosemary Richey, Germany; Joanna Steporowska, Poland; Chris Turner, Spain; Anne Weber, Switzerland; Bob Wright, France.

Picture research and permissions by Hilary Fletcher
Text permissions by Viv Tweed
Production Controller: Clive Rumble
Recording produced by James Richardson at The Soundhouse. Sound engineer: Phil Horne
Interviews by Suzie Fairfax with Andy Parsons, Rachel Babington, Ralph Jackson, Kristi O'Brien and Sue Hill
Book design and make-up by Hardlines.
Illustrations by Bill Piggins
Concept and cover design by Andrew Oliver

And thanks most of all to:
Charlotte Adams
and Jane Coates

Acknowledgements

The author and publishers are grateful to the following for permission to use copyright material in *Making Progress*. While every effort has been made, it has not been possible to identify the sources of all the material used and in such cases the publishers would welcome information from the copyright owners:

for the Dictionary extracts on p. 13 from the *Cambridge Advanced Learner's Dictionary* (2003), edited by Patrick Gillard, published by Cambridge University Press; for the cover on p. 14 of *Strengthen your memory*, by Michael Fidlow, reproduced by permission of the publisher, W. Foulsham & Co Ltd.; for the cover on p. 14 of *Improve your memory*, Fourth Edition © 2000, by Ron Fry. Published by Career Press, Franklin Lakes, NJ, USA; for the text on p. 26, 'Falling in love', from 'Kids say the darndest things', with kind permission of Edward Goss, Publisher of *The On-line Joke Book*, www.onlinejokebook.com; for the article on p. 32, 'Visiting the USA: Dos & Don'ts', reproduced with permission from USA 1, © 1999, Lonely Planet Publications; Will Hodgkinson for the text, 'Resonance' on p. 40, first published in the *Guardian* on 13 January 2003; for the article on p. 62, 'New El Niño to bring weather chaos', by J. Vidal & P. Brown, the *Guardian*, 14 January 2002, and the extract on p. 114 from 'How to use a lift' by Guy Browning, published in the *Guardian* on 22 February 2003, ©; for the information on p. 66, with kind permission of The Eden Project; for the article on p. 70, 'Wham-O', with kind permission of Veronica Howell; for the article, 'My week', on p. 88, with kind permission of Sarah Hall, first published in the *Guardian*, 13 December 2002; for the text on pp. 90 and 93, 'What is Congestion Charging?', with permission of Transport for London; for the extract on p. 98, 'Finding the bodies: real stories, real people, from *World History for Dummies* ® by Peter Haugen. Copyright © 2001 by Wiley Publishing, Inc. All rights reserved. Reproduced here by permission of the Publisher; for the extract on p. 106 from *Jojo's Story* (2004), by Antoinette Moses, and the extract from *East 43rd Street* (2001), by Alan Battersby, published by Cambridge University Press; for the extract on p. 106 from *A series of Unfortunate Events: The Bad Beginning*, by Lemony Snicket, published by HarperCollins Children's Books; for the story on p. 135, 'ATM Gives Out Free Cash', and for the story on p. 140, 'Police Use Special Cars to Catch Car Thieves', reprinted with permission of The Associated Press.

The publishers are grateful to the following for permission to reproduce copyright photographs and material:

Key: l = left, c = centre, r = right, t = top, b = bottom, back = background.

Aquarius/©New Line Cinema for p. 38 (l), /Twentieth Century Fox/Lucas Film/Gary Kurtz for p. 82 (l); Associated Press, AP/Frank Augstein for p. 100 (l), /Al Grillo for p. 100 (r); ©Anthony Blake/Anthony Blake Photo Library for p. 49; Reprinted with the permission of the publisher, from *Improve Your Memory*, Fourth Edition ©2000 Ron Fry. Published by Career Press, Franklin Lakes, NJ. All rights reserved. For p. 14; CartoonStock/©Grizelda for p. 59, /©Pete Canary for p. 11, /©Mike Baldwin for pp. 12 (l), 19, 27, 45, 92 (b), 99, 103 (b), 112 (tc), /©Kes for p. 12 (r), /©NAF for pp. 15, 112 (tl), /©Jorodo for pp. 24 (b), 30 (b), 35, 39, 71, 75 (b), 89, 107, 111, /©Stan Eales for p. 37, /©Cathy Thorne for p. 42 (b), ©Robert Thompson for pp. 48 (b), 63 (b), /©Adey Bryant for pp. 53, 144, /©Martin Guhl for pp. 54, 78 (b), /©Patrick Hardin for p. 67 (b), /©John West for p. 84 (b), /©Mike Williams for p. 112 (tr); ©CORBIS for p. 136 (r), /©James Randklev for p. 36 (tr), /©Nancy Kaszerman/ZUMA for p. 38 (r), /©Ed Quinn for p. 44, /©Dave G.Houser for pp. 46 (l), 56 (r), /©Adam Woolfitt for p. 56 (l), /©Charles O'Rear for p. 56 (cl), /SABA/©James Leynse for p. 63 (tl), /SYGMA/©Allen Martin for p. 63 (tr), /©Kevin Schafer for p. 64 (tl), /©Michael Boys for p. 64 (tr), /©Tom Grill for p. 68 (r), /©Reg Charity for p. 96 (r), /©Claudia Kunin for p. 110 (b4); ©Diverse Travel www.diversetravel.com.au for p. 58 (t, br); Dogs Today reproduced with permission of *Dogs Today* for p. 104; Total Film ©Future Publishing for p. 104; GettyImages/ImageBank/Blue Lemon Productions for p. 94, /Andy Bullock for p. 10 (l), /Marina Jefferson for p. 10 (r), /Romilly Lockyer for p. 42 (1), /Daly & Newton for p. 42 (2), /Color Day Production for p. 42 (4), /Britt Erlanson for p. 48 (c), /Peter Hendrie for p. 56 (cr), /Yellow Dog Productions for p. 74 (l), /Elyse Lewin for p. 96 (l), /Larry Dale Gordon for p. 108 (l), /Daniel

Acknowledgements continued

Arsenault for p. 110 (tl); GettyImages/Hulton Archive/Express for p. 82 (r); GettyImages/PhotoDisc/Steve Mason for p. 92 (t), /SW Productions for p. 108 (r), /PhotoDisc Collection for p. 115; GettyImages/Photographers Choice/Elyse Lewin for p. 32; GettyImages/Stone/David Schultz for p. 60, /Peter Cade for p. 18, /Michael Rosenfeld for p. 20 (r), /Ian Shaw for p. 42 (3), /David Roth for p. 42 (5), /Thomas Hoeffgen for p. 68 (l), /Dennis Kitchen for p. 70 (r), /Donna Day for p. 74 (r), /Gandee Vasan for p. 84 (t), /David Fraser for p. 86 (l), /©Ed Pritchard for p. 90, /Darryl Torckler for p. 102, /Cat Gwynn for p. 110 (t3), /Darren Robb for pp. 110 (b1, b3), /Jerome Tisne for p. 110 (b2); GettyImages/Taxi/V.C.L for p. 8, /Barry Yee for p. 16 (l), /Antonio Mo for pp. 16 (r), 30 (l), /S.Benbow for p. 20 (l), /John Lawlor for p. 22, /Stephen Simpson for p. 24 (t), /Justin Pumfrey for p. 30 (r), /Jon Arnold for p. 36 (tl), /Adrian Lyon for p. 36 (b), /Erin Patrice O'Brien for p. 68 (c), /John Giustina for p. 70 (l), /Bob Peterson for p. 86 (r), /Dick Luria for p. 108 (c), /Darren Robb for p. 110 (t2), /Nick White for p. 110 (t4), /Ron Chapple for p. 135, /Karen Moskowitz for p. 136 (l); Ronald Grant Archive for pp. 132, 138; ©*Guardian*/Graham Turner for p. 40 (t); ©HONDA/Paul Zak for p. 67 (t); ©IKEA for p. 34; World Soccer ©IPC Media for p. 104; ©Leo Jones for pp. 9, 33, 46, 52, 55, 66, 143; PA Photos/Stefan Rousseau for p. 103 (t); ©Puzzler Media Limited, *Puzzler Magazine* for p. 104; ©Resonance 104.4 FM for p. 40 (b); With thanks to Royal Mail for p. 88; ©*The Beano* ©D.C.Thomson & Co., Ltd for p. 104; US Library of Congress/Sergei Mikhailovich Prokudin-Gorskii for p. 98; ©Wayward Bus Company www.waywardbus.com.au for p. 58 (bl); ©*Your Health Plus* 2004 for p. 104; ©zefa/creasource for p. 48 (r).

We have been unable to trace the copyright owner of the photograph on page 70 (l) and would appreciate any information to enable us to do so.

Welcome!

The **Student's Book** contains 24 units, each in two parts. Each unit is based on a different topic, and each part covers a different aspect of the topic.

Part A contains three sections:

Speaking and Vocabulary

Grammar practice

Vocabulary development or Pronunciation

Part B contains three sections:

Reading and/or Listening

Writing

Speaking

After every five units there is a **Revision unit**, which revises the vocabulary, grammar and pronunciation from the previous five units. There are puzzles and exercises to help you to remember what you learnt.

Speaking Discussions give you a chance to practise using English and help you to become more confident in speaking English. In most of the Speaking activities you'll be working in pairs or in groups. It's important to use English all the time when you're working with partners – because the only way to improve your spoken English is by *speaking* it!

The speech balloons give you useful phrases to help you to speak in a clear, polite and friendly way.

Communication activities In some Speaking activities each person looks at different information. The Communication activities are printed on separate pages (pages 131 to 143) so that you can't read each other's information and a natural conversation develops between you.

Listening The recordings for *Making Progress* include many different voices speaking at their natural speed. The tasks in the book help you to understand the main points the speakers make.

Vocabulary New words are introduced in the Vocabulary exercises, and also indirectly through the activities and exercises. When you come across a useful new word or expression in the book, why not highlight it using a fluorescent highlighter? This will help you to remember the new words you meet.

Reading The Reading texts have questions to help you to understand them, learn more vocabulary and then discuss the topic.

Writing The Writing tasks will help you to improve your writing skills.

Grammar reference Pages 118 to 130 explain the main 'problem areas' of English grammar with rules and examples.

Thank you for reading this introduction. Enjoy *Making Progress!*

You and me

What sort of person are you?

a London bus

a New York taxi

the sky

a penguin

a leaf

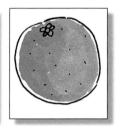
an orange

1 👥 Work in pairs. What's wrong with the pictures?

> *If it's a London bus, it shouldn't be yellow, it should be . . .*

What are these colours called? Fill the gaps:

m *aroon*   **a** _____   **b** _____   **m** _____   **o** _____   **p** _____   **t** _____ **t** _____

2 🔊 Listen to Anna and Max – what are their favourite colours?

ANNA likes 5 colours: ....

and doesn't like 2 colours: ....

MAX likes 3 colours: ....

and doesn't like 4 colours: ....

👥 Number these colours in your own order of preference (1 to 10):

B   **B**   **B**   **G**   **P**   **P**   **R**   **W**   **Y**   **G**

3 👥 + 👥 Join another pair and look at **Communication Activity 1** on page 131. Find out what your choices say about your personalities.

4 🔊 Listen to the recording and follow the instructions. You'll need a clean sheet of paper and a pencil.

👥 Look at **Activity 21** on page 136. Find out what your drawing says about your personality!

5 👥 Decide which FIVE adjectives best describe your own personality – and your partner's personality.

active	easy-going	happy	lively	sociable
calm	forgetful	hard-working	open-minded	strict
careful	funny	helpful	relaxed	thoughtful
careless	generous	kind	serious	tolerant
considerate	gentle	lazy	shy	unkind

Present simple and past simple

1 First look at the examples in the Grammar reference section on page 119.

2 Fill the gaps in these sentences:

> The Grammar reference sections give a short summary of grammar rules and examples. You can refer to these rules at any time if you have any doubts.

1 I usually ....*go*........ to bed around midnight and ....*fall*.... asleep very quickly.
Yesterday I .... to bed at 11, but I .... asleep until 12.

2 Water .... at 100° Celsius, and .... at 0°.
The temperature .... so low last night that the lake ....
If you .... ice it melts and .... water.

3 Usually he .... to work by bus, but yesterday he .... by car.

3 Complete these sentences:

1 Usually I .... for breakfast, but today I ....
What .... you .... ?

2 If someone is rude to me I .... If someone is kind to me I .... If someone gives me a present I ....

3 The last time someone was rude to me I .... The last time someone was kind to me I .... The last time someone gave me a present I ....

4 Work in groups of three or four. Ask each other these questions:

> *What do you usually do on Sundays?*
> *... on Saturday evenings?*
> *... on Mondays?*

> *What did you do last Sunday?*
> *... last Saturday evening?*
> *... last Monday?*

Numbers

1 What are these numbers? Say each one aloud.

2 Listen to the recording and fill the gaps. Then take turns to say the sentences aloud.

> Say numbers clearly and slowly so that people can easily understand you.

1 My telephone number is ....
The moon is .... kilometres from the Earth.

2 My passport number is ....
The deepest part of the Pacific Ocean is .... metres deep.

3 Their car registration number is JG ....
The height of Mount Everest is .... metres.

4 The price of this CD is £ .... 74.95 divided by 5 equals ....

5 $1\frac{1}{4}$ multiplied by 3 is .... 5 times 0.75 is ....

3 Write down these numbers, then dictate them to your partner:

Two telephone numbers   A passport or ID card number
The prices of the last two things you bought   A car registration number
Another number that is important to you

1B Family and friends

Just relax

1 👥 **Look at the photos and discuss these questions:**

- Which person above is more like you?
- Which members of your family are often stressed? Which are usually relaxed?
- How many of your friends suffer from stress?
- What do you do to relax?

2 **Read the advice below before you hear the recording.**

🔊 **Listen to the recording and tick ✓ the advice that the speakers gave:**

1 One minute of laughter is as good as 45 minutes of exercise. ☐

2 Ten minutes stroking an animal will reduce blood pressure. If you don't have a pet, borrow one. ☐

3 Make a list. Write down ten things that make you happy and incorporate them into your daily life. ☐

4 Do some exercise. A bit of movement not only relieves stress but can also increase concentration and give you a general feeling of well-being. ☐

5 Eating little and often helps keep blood sugar levels up. ☐

6 Walking is both a relaxing form of exercise and gives you a chance to think. ☐

7 Breathe in. Take twenty deep breaths ten times a day to balance and replenish body and mind. ☐

8 Walk tall. A good posture means your body feels fewer ill effects when it is tense. ☐

9 Put your fingers in your ears and close your eyes. Listen to your inner sounds for a few minutes and relax. ☐

10 Have a haircut – a quick way to feel (and look) better. ☐

11 Don't be afraid to spend time alone. It's an important way to take stock of the day's events. ☐

12 Spend time with a friend. Make dinner or just have a good chat. ☐

13 Have a good stretch. Roll your shoulders and wiggle your fingers. ☐

3 👥👥 **Discuss these questions:**

- Which of the advice above do you agree with?
- Which do you disagree with?
- Can you suggest more tips to help each other to relax?

Writing to a friend

1 👥 Read this e-mail from your friend Alex.

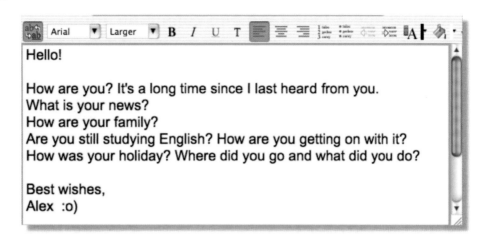

Hello!

How are you? It's a long time since I last heard from you.
What is your news?
How are your family?
Are you still studying English? How are you getting on with it?
How was your holiday? Where did you go and what did you do?

Best wishes,
Alex :o)

2 👥 Before you write a reply, decide what you will say to Alex.

3 ✎ Write your reply to Alex.

4 👥 Show your reply to a partner, and read his or her reply.

Likes and dislikes

1 🔊 Practise saying these phrases:

What is your favourite . . . ?
Do you like . . . ?
Why do you like . . . so much ?
What . . . do you dislike most ?
Why don't you like . . . ?

Well, I do like . . . but I think I like . . . more.
I don't really have a favourite, but I do like . . . a lot.
Because . . .
That's hard to say, but I don't like . . . very much.
I'm not sure really.
What about you? What's your favourite . . . ?

2 👥 Fill this chart with your partner's favourites:

	favourite	least favourite
colour		
car		
band		
game		
fruit		
language		
TV show		
book		
film star		

3 👥 + 👥 Join another pair. Tell them what you found out.

What likes and dislikes do you have in common?

The English language

Talking about language and communication

'This is delicious. I'm glad I didn't try to order in Italian.'

'Oops! Silly me. Here's what I should have told you to ask. . .'

1 👥 **Look at the cartoons and discuss these questions:**

- When are phrase books and dictionaries misleading – or even dangerous?
- When have you been misunderstood? What happened?

2 👥 **Match these terms to the words in red in this story. You can use a term more than once.**

adjective
adverb
article
italics
modal verb
noun
paragraph
phrasal verb
phrase
preposition
sentence
verb

Mrs Duncan had done her shopping at the supermarket. She got back to her car in the car park, and found four young men in the car. She screamed at them at the top of her voice, 'Get out of the car! I have a gun and I know how to use it!' The four men jumped out of the car and ran like mad. She loaded her shopping bags into the back of the car and got into the driver's seat. But her key wouldn't fit the ignition. This was when she realized that this couldn't be her car. *Her* car was parked in the next row. She put her stuff into her own car and drove quickly to the police station. She felt guilty and wanted to explain her terrible mistake.

She told her story to the sergeant at the desk. He pointed to the other end of the counter where four pale young men had just reported that a mad woman had stolen their car.

Mrs Duncan apologized to them. They saw the funny side of it – eventually. (She didn't really have a gun.)

3 👥 **Fill the gaps in these sentences, using a dictionary if necessary.**

1 *a, e, i, o* and *u* are all ....
2 All the other letters of the .... (*b, c, d,* etc.) are ....
3 An English-to-English dictionary doesn't .... words, it explains them and gives ....
4 People from different regions speak with different ....
5 You can learn more from someone's .... (a smile, a frown, etc.) than from their words.
6 He gave us a thumbs-up .... to show everything was OK.

4 👥👥 **Discuss these questions:**

- What languages would you like to learn? Why?
- Why do you think it's useful to learn foreign languages?
- How many people in the world speak your own language?

Prepositions – 1

1 First look _at_ the Grammar reference section _on_ page 119.

2 👥 Fill the gaps _in_ this story:

Four American bank managers flew _to_ Australia to take part _in_ a golf tournament. They all had bright green jackets .... the name .... their bank .... large letters .... the back. .... the tournament they had a day free, so they decided to rent a car and drive .... the city. They drove .... the country, hoping to see some kangaroos.

But they were .... luck. .... driving .... hours, they didn't see a single kangaroo. So they turned the car around and started to drive back .... the city. .... that very moment a kangaroo hopped .... the road directly .... front .... them, and they hit the poor animal. It landed .... a thud .... the road. Dead, they thought.

Then one .... the bankers had the bright idea .... putting his green jacket .... the kangaroo and taking some photos of it .... his friends .... their green jackets. So they lifted up the kangaroo and dressed it .... the jacket. Then they stood .... the kangaroo while they took photos .... each other.

But the kangaroo wasn't dead. It opened its eyes, jumped .... the air, and hopped away .... the distance, still wearing the jacket. Soon it was .... sight.

Unfortunately the key .... the car was .... the pocket .... that green jacket. And all .... their airline tickets and their passports!

Using a dictionary

1 👥 Look at these phrases from the story on page 12. Which of the meanings of at are explained in the dictionary? Write the number of each meaning.

at the supermarket .....1..... She screamed **at** them ....

at the top of her voice .... the sergeant **at** the desk ....

2 👥 Look at these examples of about. Which of the meanings are explained in the dictionary? Write the number of each meaning.

He told us about his holiday.	about[1]	....
What about having a drink?	about[1]	....
What about you – did you have a good holiday?	about[1]	....
What was the film about?	about[1]	....
He walked about the city taking photos.	about[1]	....
I was about to phone you when you phoned me.	about[2]	....
We got back about three weeks ago.	about[2]	....

• asymmetry /eɪˈsɪmɪtri/ *noun* [U]

ᴼ⁻**at** *strong form* /æt/ *weak form* /ət/ *preposition*
1 [PLACE] used to show the place or position of something or someone *We met at the station.* • *She was sitting at the table.* • *She's at the library.* **2** [TIME] used to show the time something happens *The meeting starts at three.* **3** [DIRECTION] towards or in the direction of *She threw the ball at him.* • *He's always shouting at the children.* **4** [ABILITY] used after an adjective to show a person's ability to do something *He's good at making friends.* • *I've always been useless at tennis.* **5** [CAUSE] used to show the cause of something, especially a feeling *We were surprised at the news.* **6** [AMOUNT] used to show the price, speed, level, etc of something *He denied driving at 120 miles per hour.* **7** [ACTIVITY] used to show a state or activity *She was hard at work when I arrived.* • *a country at war* **8** [INTERNET] the @ symbol, used in email addresses to separate the name of a person, department, etc from the name of the organization or company
ate /eɪt, et/ *past tense of* eat

the change of leadership.

ᴼ⁻**about**[1] /əˈbaʊt/ *preposition* **1** relating to a particular subject or person *a book about the Spanish Civil War* • *What was she talking about?* **2** UK (US **around**) to or in different parts of a place, often without purpose or order *They were creeping about the garden.* • *We heard someone moving about outside.* **3 what/how about ...?** **a** used to make a suggestion *How about France for a holiday?* **b** used to ask for someone's opinion on a particular subject *What about Ann – is she nice?*
ᴼ⁻**about**[2] /əˈbaʊt/ *adv* **1** [APPROXIMATELY] used before a number or amount to mean approximately *It happened about two months ago.* **2** [DIRECTION] UK (US **around**) to or in different parts of a place, often without purpose or order *She's always leaving her clothes lying about.* **3** [NEAR] UK informal (US **around**) If someone or something is about, they are near to the place where you are now. *Is Kate about?* **4 be about to do sth** to be going to do something very soon *I stopped her just as she was about to leave.*
ᴼ⁻**above**[1] /əˈbʌv/ *adv, preposition* **1** [HIGHER]

Find out more @ http://dictionary.cambridge.org

2B A better memory?

Can you remember?

1 👥 Test your memory! Do you remember . . .

- Your best friend's phone number? And his or her birthday?
- The name of your country's president? The name of the American President?
- The title of the last book you read? The name of the author?
- The title of the last movie you saw? The names of two of the stars?
- What a cinema ticket costs?
- The name of the woman in the story on page 12?
- The name of your first teacher? The name of your first English teacher?

How quickly did you remember all that information?

2 👥 **Which of these things do you find easy to remember? Number them in order of difficulty (10 = very difficult, 1 = quite easy).**

.... people's names	.... where you put things
.... the tunes of songs	.... phone numbers
.... addresses	.... spellings
.... times of appointments or classes	.... English grammar rules
.... English vocabulary	.... funny stories

3 👥 **Look at some information about two books. Which book looks better? Why?**

A SELF-IMPROVEMENT COURSE
YOU ALREADY KNOW
THAT YOUR MEMORY IS SUSPECT!

This book will change that. In your hands you hold
the key to a new, reliable and dynamic memory.

Here you will learn about your real potential and be taught the classic
memory methods which have been used to such good effect by
successful men and women around the world.

You will be able to remember numbers, people, jokes, facts, foreign
languages and much more information gained from everyday reading.
All you have to do is learn how.

You have two kinds of memory:

Natural and Artificial. You can strengthen both. It's not even difficult –
you just have to commit yourself to this book and let it teach you how
to re-organize your thinking. Do that and practise the simple
exercises and, in a very short time, you won't remember what it was
like to forget anything!

Many people believe that they have a
poor memory, even more wish they
were capable of remembering more.
This practical text gives proven tips on
how anyone can improve the power of
their memory. With advice on
improving recollection of names, dates,
facts and formulae, this guide even
shows how to improve spelling. It also
includes simple tests to check that the
memory rules are really sinking in.

4 👥 **Highlight the words in the texts that mean the same as these phrases:**

can't be trusted	decide to learn from
dependable	tested
obtained	memory
make stronger	being remembered

 Find out more @
www.amazon.co.uk

Punctuation

1 First look at the Grammar reference section on page 120.

2 🔊 Listen to the recording and add the punctuation marks to this story. Some gaps need more than one punctuation mark.

Two students taking a chemistry class at the university were doing well in class .... they were sure they would get an 'A' grade in the final exam .... Because they were so confident .... they decided to drive to another city the night before the exam to have a party with some friends ....

Unfortunately .... they got back too late to take their exam .... So they found their professor and said to him ....

.... We....re very sorry we missed the exam .... Our car had a flat tyre ....

.... OK.... you can take the exam tomorrow ....

.... Thanks .... Professor ....

The next day the professor placed them in separate rooms.... handed each a test booklet .... and told them to begin .... Opening the booklets .... the students found just one question ....

.... Which tyre ....

3 ✎ Rewrite this text, adding punctuation and capital letters:

remembering english vocabulary

there are many different ways of helping yourself to remember vocabulary one method is to highlight each new word you see in this book writing words down in a notebook is also a good idea if you do this write a sentence using the new word not just a translation if you have a vocabulary notebook arrange it so that you have a new page for each different topic when using a dictionary make sure you look at the examples not just the definitions

Ideas and reasons

1 🔊 👥 Listen to the recording and say the phrases aloud. Try to copy the intonation.

Bob writes new words in a notebook.
— That sounds like a good idea.
Why do you think so?
— Because ...
Oh yes, I see what you mean.

— Susan repeats new words over and over.
That doesn't sound like a good idea.
— Why not?
Because ...
— Well, I see what you mean. But ...

2 👥👥 Two of you should look at **Activity 2** on page 131, the other(s) at **Activity 22** on page 137. Follow the instructions there.

'Sorry it's late. I forgot'

Shops and shopping

Going shopping

Topic vocabulary

1 👥 **Look at the photos and discuss these questions:**

- Do you enjoy shopping? Why/Why not?
- What are your three favourite shops? Why?
- Which shops do you hate going into? Why?
- What do you like and dislike about:

  a supermarkets **b** department stores **c** shopping malls **d** street markets?

2 👥 **Look at these pictures. Match the words to the pictures.**

> belt boots buttons coat collar cuff dress gloves hat heel jacket jeans
> neck pocket sandals scarf shirt shoes skirt sleeve socks sweater
> sweatshirt tie tights trainers trousers underwear zip

3 👥 **Which words are not illustrated? Show what they mean by pointing to your own clothes.**

4 👥 **Choose the best word from below to fit in each gap.**

1 The price was €5.50 – I gave the man at the .... a €20 .... but he only gave me €4.50 ....

2 How much does she .... a week – what's her annual ....?
How much .... does she give her son a week?

3 He .... all day .... , and he didn't use his .... at all and the only .... he .... was for some snacks in the ....

> cash   cash desk   change   credit card   earn/get paid   market   note
> pocket-money/allowance   salary/pay   spent   spent   window-shopping

Articles and quantifiers – 1

1 First look at the examples in the Grammar reference section on page 120.

2 👥 Fill each gap in these stories with: **a   each   his   many   much   some** or **the** Leave the gaps blank where no article is needed.

> **1** .... man in .... Florida stopped .... motorist and said he had .... gun. He forced her to drive to .... nearest cash machine. Then .... man withdrew .... money from .... own bank account.
>
> **2** .... man walked into .... shop in .... Illinois and asked for all .... money in .... cash drawer. But there was not very .... money in .... drawer, so he tied up .... assistant and worked at .... counter himself for three hours until .... police arrived and caught him.
>
> **3** Police in .... Los Angeles had .... good luck with .... robbery suspect who just couldn't control himself during .... line-up. When .... detective asked .... man in .... line-up to repeat .... words, 'Give me all .... money or I'll shoot,' he shouted, 'That's not what I said!'
>
> **4** In .... California .... man was arrested for trying to hold up .... bank without .... weapon. He used .... thumb and .... finger to simulate .... gun, but unfortunately he forgot to keep .... hand in .... pocket.

3 👥 Fill the gaps in these sentences:

1 'How .... of the stories really happened?'
'................ of the stories are true, and .... are invented.'

2 'How .... time did it take you to finish the exercise?'
'It didn't take me as .... minutes as I expected.'

3 'Which of .... criminals in .... stories was .... most stupid?'

Vowels – 1

1 🔊 Listen to the recording and say these words aloud.

feel · fill   send · sand   ran · run   dock · duck   ham · harm   full · fool
short · shot   turn · torn

2 🔊 Listen to the recording and write down the words you hear:

w........	s........	b........	h........	m........	j........
w........	s........	b........	h........	m........	j........
	s........	b........	h........	m........	j........
	s........	b........			j........

Look at **Activity 43** to see the correct answers. Then say all the words aloud.

3 🔊 Listen to the recording and fill the gaps. Then take turns to read these sentences aloud.

1 iː ɪ   Does J................ support the same t................ as T................ and J................?

2 æ ʌ   Isn't H................ a l................ m................? Yes, but D................ is h................ .

3 e æ   F................ and H................ are J................'s b................ f................ .

4 ʊ uː   Don't be s................ a f................! Don't j................ into the p................! It isn't f................!

5 ɔː ɜː   Do you w................ to w................? Or do you pre................ a sh................ bus ride?

6 ɔː ɒ   G................ loves s................ . J................ likes in................ h................ .

Spend or save?

How much did you spend?

1 👥 **Look at the photo:**

- What is everyone wearing?
- What are they saying to each other? What would you say to them?

2 🔊 **You'll hear interviews with Julie (in the middle), Bill (behind), David (on the left) and Teresa (on the right). Fill the chart with the information they give.**

		JULIE		BILL		DAVID		TERESA	
prices paid	polo shirt	£..........	t-shirt	£..........	jeans	£..........	shorts	£..........
	shorts	£..........	CDs	£..........	trainers	£..........	sandals	£..........
	shoes	£..........	batteries	£..........	sweatshirt	£..........	sunglasses	£..........
full prices	polo shirt	£..........	t-shirt	£..........	jeans	£..........	shorts	£..........
	shorts	£..........	CDs	£..........	trainers	£..........	sandals	£..........
	shoes	£..........	batteries	£..........	sweatshirt	£..........	sunglasses	£..........
total spent		£..........		£..........		£..........		£..........
total saved		£..........		£..........		£..........		£..........

3 👥👥 **Discuss these questions:**

- Do you look for bargains, like the people in the interviews? Where do you find them?
- Who do you go shopping with?
- What do you like to buy?

Giving your opinion

1 🔊 👥 Listen to the recording and say the phrases aloud.

> *It seems to me that . . .*   — *what do you think?*
> *I believe that . . .*   — *do you agree?*
> *Do you agree that . . . ?*
> *Don't you agree that . . . ?*

> *I think so too.*
> *No, I don't agree at all.*
> *No, not really. I think that . . .*
> *Sure, yes. I agree completely.*

2 👥👥 Take turns to give your opinion about each of these topics and find out if your partners agree.

> *It seems to me that . . .*   *giving money to charity is . . .*
> *I believe that . . .*   **giving money to beggars is . . .**
> *Do you agree that . . .*   *buying lottery tickets is . . .*
> *Don't you agree that . . . ?*   **tipping people who serve you is . . .**
>   *putting money in the bank is . . .*
>   **borrowing money from friends is . . .**
>   *window-shopping is . . .*
>   **buying only designer clothes is . . .**
>   *buying only second-hand clothes is . . .*
>   **keeping up with fashion is . . .**
>   *throwing away old clothes is . . .*
>   **spending all your money on clothes is . . .**

3 👥 Look at these two paragraphs. Which is better? Why?

Money can't buy happiness.

If you have a lot of money you can buy whatever you want. This means that if you want a new pair of shoes you can buy them without worrying about the cost. Or you can travel anywhere in the world and stay in the most expensive hotels. I don't think this would make me happy.

Why do people gamble?

People who go to casinos or bet on horse races say, 'It's fun! It's exciting! It's wonderful to win!' But gamblers don't usually win – they lose most of the time. Even if they lose enormous amounts of money they still go on gambling. Why? Because gambling is like a drug, and it's very hard to give it up once you're addicted. And, like a drug, it can be an expensive habit.

4 👥 You find a wallet in the street, take it to the police station and leave your name and address. One month later a cheque for £100 comes in the post – a reward from the owner. What will you do – spend it or save it?

Discuss the alternatives, then . . .

5 ✎ Write about 50 words beginning:

> *It's better to spend the money . . .*

or

> *It's better to save the money . . .*

'Just lend me a bit more. I feel lucky'

© Mike Baldwin/ Cornered

Money

4A Schools and colleges

Teaching and learning

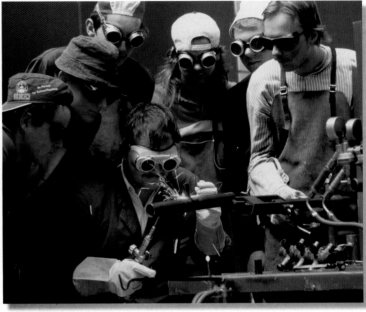

1 👥 **Look at the photos and discuss these questions:**

- Which class looks more enjoyable? Why?
- What do/did you enjoy most about school?
- Who would your ideal teacher be like?

an older brother		an older sister
an uncle	or	an aunt
a friend		a stranger
a grandfather		a grandmother?

2 👥 **Fill the gaps in these sentences with words from below:**

1   In the UK most children start .... at the age of five and move to a ....
when they are eleven. They can .... school at sixteen, but most students stay on in the
.... till they are eighteen.

2   Our teacher was very .... and we were always .... if we misbehaved. Sometimes,
if we were really ...., we were put in .... and had to stay after school.

3   The .... is in charge of the .... and .... of a school.

4   Mary got such good .... in her exams, that she got a .... at Cambridge
.... and a .... to pay for her studies. She did so well there that she ....
with first class ....

> detention graduated head honours leave marks/scores/grades naughty place
> primary school punished pupils/students scholarship secondary school sixth form
> staff strict University

3 👥👥 **Discuss these questions:**

- What is/was your favourite subject at school? Why?
- Which lessons are/were the most fun? Why?
- Should lessons be serious or fun?
- What are your educational plans for the future?

Past simple and present perfect

1 First look at the Grammar reference section on page 121.

2 🔢 Spot the mistakes in these sentences and correct them:
1 When has she left school? Did she start university already?
2 He has started school when he has been five.
3 I enjoyed learning English but I didn't finish learning yet.

3 🔢 Complete these sentences:

1 'What .... on Saturday?'
'I .... to town and .... some shopping.'
2 'What .... so far today?'
'I .... to class and I .... doing this exercise.'
3 '................ you ever .... the USA?'
'Yes, I .... there two years ago. I .... a wonderful time.'
4 When she .... younger, she .... the piano. But she
.... playing two years ago and she ....n't .... since then.

4 🔢 + 🔢 Compare your answers. Then find out what the others did last weekend – and how many times they've done the same things so far this year.

> *What did you do in the morning?*
> *What else did you do?*

> *What did you do after that?*
> *Have you done that a lot this year?*

Collocations – 1

1 🔢 Which **verb** is missing from each of these phrases?

👁 Collocations are words that usually go together, like *a bad cold* or *a bad temper*.

1 .... a break .... an exam .... a look .... an interest
2 .... a letter .... a book .... your name .... an essay

Which **adjective** is missing from these phrases?

3 a .... cold .... traffic .... rain a .... suitcase
4 a .... success a .... idea a .... many with .... difficulty
5 a .... portion a .... child a .... apartment a .... car

2 🔢 Look at these collocations. Then use them in the sentences below:

make	a living	**do**	100 kph	**a good**	chance
	a mistake		a job		cook
	a noise		someone a favour		example
	a promise		the cooking		time
	a request		the washing-up		day
	a suggestion		well in her exam		mood
	an appointment		your homework		temper
	friends		the work		reason

1 'This exercise is really difficult.'
'Can I .... a ....? Let's .... it together.'
2 If you want to see the doctor you have to ....
3 'Shall we have a meal at my place? I'm quite a ....'
'OK. If you ...., I'll .... afterwards.'
4 'How many .... did you .... in the test?'
'Not too many. That's because I .... plenty of .... before.'
5 It's not easy for some people to .... new ....
6 There's a .... that she'll .... in her exam.
7 We all had a .... at the party and everyone was in a ....

4B Happy days?

My education

1 We asked David, 19, and his sister Sally, 17, to write about their school-days. Read their stories and then put ticks in the chart below:

My name's David. I started school when I was five years old. I enjoyed my time at primary school, made lots of new friends and learnt to read and write and do arithmetic.

But when I was eleven my family moved to another part of the city and I had to leave all my friends who went to a different secondary school. It was scary being in a new school with hundreds of older and bigger children I didn't know. But my new class teacher was Mrs Green and she was wonderful – she really helped me feel more secure in my new environment. And she made us all work really hard too!

After working hard for the first year with Mrs Green's encouragement, I realized I didn't need to do so much work, so I didn't make much effort in any classes, because I found everything quite easy. I know this was stupid but none of the teachers pushed me to do better so I just did the minimum amount of work necessary.

When I took my GCSEs at the age of sixteen my results were really poor. That taught me a good lesson and since then I haven't been so lazy!

Now I'm studying history at uni.

I'm Sally. Like David, I was eleven when I went to secondary school. At first I had a really hard time because, although I did have two good friends, some of the other children picked on me and teased me because I was quite small for my age. My reaction to this was to be naughty in class and cheeky to the teachers and this got me into trouble – I was in detention a lot.

This went on for a couple of years until I became more confident. I decided to work hard to show the others that I was better than them. The trouble was that despite my hard work I didn't do very well in tests and still got bad reports from the teachers. So I really didn't like school, and I stopped making an effort.

But now I'm in the sixth form, everything is different. I'm interested in the subjects I'm doing, the teachers all treat us like adults and (fingers crossed!) I hope to do well in my exams at the end of the year.

If I get the grades I'm hoping for, I'm going to take a gap year before starting university in two years' time.

	David	Sally
Didn't work hard all the time	☐	☐
Found it hard to make new friends	☐	☐
Was not encouraged by the teachers	☐	☐
Got bad test or exam results	☐	☐
Got into trouble	☐	☐
Was teased	☐	☐
Now works harder	☐	☐

2 🔊 Now you'll hear two different people (Andy and Rachel) talking about their school-days. Put ticks in the chart with information about them.

	Andy	Rachel
Didn't like maths or science	☐	☐
Enjoyed outdoor activities	☐	☐
Had to make friends at secondary school	☐	☐
Has a twin brother	☐	☐
Liked English, geography and history	☐	☐
Played tricks on people	☐	☐

Making notes

1 👥 Look at the notes David and Sally made before they wrote their stories. Whose notes do you prefer? Which two points did they each not include in their final stories?

Primary School (5) - had fun + learnt a lot

Secondary School (11) - difficult hard time

Others bullied teased me (small for my age!) naughty + cheeky ⟶ detention

13: more confident ⟶ worked hard to impress others ⟶ unsuccessful!

Me: bad at tests + poor reports

6th form: better! Interested + teachers don't treat us like children adults!!

Success in exams - hopefully!!!

If good grades: gap year (1st get job, then travel)

Then Uni in 2 years

PRIMARY SCHOOL (5): lots of new friends

SECONDARY SCHOOL (11): new part of city + left old friends + big school v. worrying

Mrs Green: security + worked hard

Then ... other teachers: no encouragement I didn't work

played football for school team

GCSES: v. poor results!

Then ... worked harder

(was house captain in last year.)

Now Uni: history

👁

'Why bother to make notes before writing?' Because notes help you to . . .

1 Organize your thoughts and ideas.
2 Plan what points you want to make.
3 Decide which points to leave out if there's not enough time or space.
4 Arrange your points in the best order.
5 Remember your ideas while you're writing.

2 ✏️ Imagine you are going to move to another school. Write about 100 words telling your new teacher about your education so far.

Agreeing and disagreeing

1 🔊 👥 Listen to the recording and say the phrases aloud:

> I agree with that.
> That's absolutely right.
> I quite agree.

> I don't really agree.
> I don't think so.
> I don't think that's right.

> I don't really know.
> I can't make up my mind.
> I'm really not sure.

2 👥👥👥 Find out who agrees or disagrees with each opinion. Use the phrases above – don't just say 'Yes' or 'No'. Record everyone's views on the right.

	Agree ✓ Disagree ✗ Not sure ?
There should be no private schools.	....
Boarding schools are good for children.	....
Children should start school when they are five.	....
Children should start school when they are seven.	....
School and college terms should be shorter.	....
It's OK to cheat in an exam.	....
It doesn't matter if you fail an exam.	....
Learning English is fun.	....
Learning history is a waste of time.	....
There's no point in doing any homework.	....
All students should do sport at school.	....

3

👥 Write down three more opinions about education or another subject.

👥 + 👥 Find out if the others agree or disagree with your opinions.

5A Families

Relatives

1 👥 **Look at the photo and discuss these questions:**

- Why do you think the people in the picture are celebrating?
- How many people are there in your family?
- Do you enjoy family parties? Why/Why not?

2 👥 **Look at this family tree and fill the gaps in the sentences:**

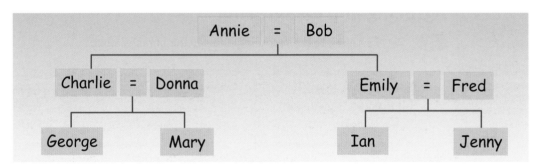

```
                    Annie  =  Bob
          ┌───────────┴────────────────┐
   Charlie = Donna              Emily = Fred
     ┌───────┴───────┐            ┌──────┴───────┐
  George        Mary           Ian          Jenny
```

1 Annie is Emily's mother – so Emily is Annie's ....

2 Fred is Annie's son-in-law – so Annie is Fred's ....

3 Donna is Ian's aunt – so Ian is Donna's ....

4 Mary is Emily's niece – so Emily is Mary's ....

5 Donna is .... to Charlie – he is her ....

6 Annie is Jenny's .... George is Ian's ....

7 Donna is Bob's ....

8 Emily and Fred are Jenny's ....

9 George and Mary are .... (they were born on the same day).

10 Who are Bob's grandsons? ....

3 👥 One of you should look at **Activity 3** on page 131, the other at **Activity 23** on page 137. You'll see another family tree there. Ask each other questions to find out the names of missing family members.

4 👥 Draw your own family tree and explain it to your partner.

5 👥 + 👥 Find out about each other's families.

'Well, you know best, Grandma. I hope you'll be very happy together.'

Modal verbs – 1

1 First look at the examples in the Grammar reference section on page 122.

2 👥 One of the words or phrases in red is wrong for each context – which is it?

It's 7.15, we .... be late for the train.	can could may
If we're very late we .... catch it.	can't may not
So, we .... be late.	can't may not mustn't
No, so we .... hurry up, then!	have to must can

3 👥 Fill the gaps with a suitable form of **can   could   have to   may   must** or **should** :

1 What time *should* .... we arrive if we want a good seat for the show?

2 You .... arrive at the last minute if you like, but I don't think you .... in case there are no seats left. And you .... leave home too late in case the traffic is bad.

3 Students .... eat in the library, but they .... drink and eat in the garden.

4 If you have to leave early you .... ask the teacher's permission.

5 '............... I leave early today? I .... go to the dentist's.'

4 👥 Think of various ways of completing these sentences:

On a plane you can't .... but you can .... and you must ....
On a bus you can't .... but you can ....
The driver of a car .... Students in our school ....

Un–, in– and im–

Is she happy?	*No she isn't, she's <u>un</u>happy!*
Is he efficient?	*Not at all, he's <u>in</u>efficient!*
Is it possible?	*No way, it's <u>im</u>possible!*

1 👥 The opposite of most adjectives is formed with *un–*, but *in–* or *im–* are used with some adjectives. Decide which of these adjectives take *un–*, *in–* or *im–*:

un able	...... efficient	...... likely	...... successful
...... capable	...... expensive	...... lucky	...... sure
...... certain	...... familiar	...... necessary	...... tidy
...... comfortable	...... formal	...... patient	...... true
...... common	...... healthy	...... pleasant	...... usual
...... convenient	...... helpful	...... polite	...... visible
...... direct	...... kind	...... probable	

2 Highlight any new words in the lists above.

3 👥 Fill the gaps in these sentences with suitable words from the list above:

1 I expected her to help me, but she was very ....

2 I couldn't walk in my new shoes – they were very ....

3 I don't expect it will rain – it's .... to rain.

4 Smoking is bad for your health – it's .... to smoke.

5 You don't need to reserve a ticket – it's .... to book.

6 There aren't many snakes in England – snakes are ....

7 I couldn't do the exercise at all – it was .... to do it.

8 Saying 'Hi!' is more .... than saying 'Good morning'.

5B Love and marriage

Falling in love

1 Read this article and then answer the questions on the next page:

A group of children (ages five to ten) in America were asked about love and marriage.

What is the best age to get married?

"Eighty-four. Because at that age, you don't have to work anymore, and you can spend all your time loving each other in your bedroom." — Judy, 8

"Once I'm done with kindergarten, I'm going to find me a wife." — Tommy, 5

What do most people do on a date?

"On the first date, they just tell each other lies, and that usually gets them interested enough to go for a second date." — Mike, 10

Is it better to be single or married?

"It's better for girls to be single, but not for boys. Boys need somebody to clean up after them." — Lynette, 9

"It gives me a headache to think about that stuff. I'm just a kid. I don't need that kind of trouble." — Kenny, 7

What is falling in love like?

"Like an avalanche where you have to run for your life." — Roger, 9

"I think you're supposed to get shot with an arrow or something, but the rest of it isn't supposed to be so painful." — Harlen, 8

"If falling in love is anything like learning to spell, I don't want to do it. It takes too long a time to learn" — Leo, 7

How important are good looks?

"If you want to be loved by somebody who isn't already in your family, it doesn't hurt to be beautiful." — Jeanne, 8

"It isn't always just how you look. Look at me. I'm handsome like anything and I haven't got anybody to marry me yet." — Gary, 7

"Beauty is skin deep. But how rich you are can last a long time" — Christine, 9

Why do lovers often hold hands?

"They want to make sure their rings don't fall off, because they paid good money for them." — David, 8

How can you make a person fall in love with you?

"One way is to take the girl out to eat. Make sure it's something she likes to eat. French fries usually works for me." — Bart, 9

How can you tell if two adults eating dinner at a restaurant are in love?

"Lovers will just be staring at each other and their food will get cold. Other people care more about the food." — Brad, 8

"Just see if the man picks up the check. That's how you can tell if he's in love." — John, 9

What are most people thinking when they say "I love you"?

"The person is thinking: Yeah, I really do love him, but I hope he showers at least once a day." — Michelle, 9

How can people make love last?

"Spend most of your time loving instead of going to work." — Tom, 7

"Be a good kisser. It might make your wife forget that you never clean your room." — Randy, 8

"Don't forget your wife's name . . . that will mess up the love." — Roger, 8

2 Find the answers to these questions:

1 How many of the children think money is important?
2 How many think food is important?
3 How many think that good looks are important?
4 How many think that males are less clean than females?
5 Which was the oldest child? Which was the youngest?

3 Highlight the words or phrases which mean the same as these:

'I have a surprise too. Until I really like a guy, I never give out my real name.'

pre-school   lots of snow falling from a mountain   good-looking (girl)
good-looking (boy)   only on the surface   spend a lot
looking hard at someone   pay the bill

4 Discuss these questions:

- Which child sounds most pessimistic?
- Who sounds the sweetest?
- Who sounds the wisest? Is it one of the older ones?
- Whose answers made you smile? Which is your favourite answer?

Short sentences, long sentences

Writing

1 Read these two stories. Choose a suitable title for each story.

Love at first sight   A love–hate relationship   Love is blind   Absence makes the heart grow fonder

Anna and Bob went to the same schools from the age of seven and even sat next to each other in most of their classes, but when they left school, Anna went to college in the USA and Bob joined the Navy and they didn't see each other again until a mutual friend's wedding some years later, and soon after that they got married themselves.

John and Mary first met on a blind date. It was a disaster. They had nothing in common. They disliked each other. Four years passed. They met again by chance. They remembered their date. They laughed about it. They had dinner. This time they got on well. They still have big arguments. John asked Mary to marry him. She hasn't said 'Yes' yet.

2 Rewrite the first story in shorter sentences.

3 Rewrite the second story, using some of these words to make longer sentences:

after   because   before   but   so   when   while

How certain are you?

1 Listen to the recording and say these phrases aloud:

Speaking

Do you think . . . ?
When do you think . . . ?
Why do you think . . . ?

Definitely.
Probably.
Possibly.
Maybe (not).
Perhaps (not).

I'm sure that . . .
I'm almost sure that . . .
I'm not sure if . . .
I don't know if . . .

2 Note down two things that may or may not happen:

today   next month
tomorrow   next year
next weekend   in the next ten years

Discuss your ideas, using the phrases above.

© Mike Baldwin / Cornered

Relationships

1–5 Revision

These revision exercises can all be done with a partner.
Or you can do them alone.

Topic vocabulary

1 There are 12 words describing personality and 7 words describing colours in this puzzle. Can you find them all?

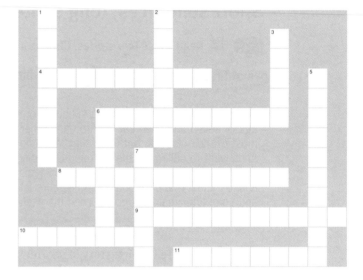

```
c r o n u r i c s y p t s u p r p o
a y s l o c b e i g e s o s a i l s
l r l i v e l y y o o t c t n p u r
m a n f o r g e t f u l i r l c m i
p o o p c o n s i d e r a t e r l a
r c a r e l e s s m l i b l u e l e
s e u o g r e e n a t o l e r a n t
o i r y e l l o w r u c e s e n s a
t u r q u o i s e o o p u r p l e a
s s o u g e n e r o u s c y r o u a
l c a r e f u l s n h e l p f u l a
g e n t l e l u t h o u g h t f u l
```

2 Read the clues and write the words in this crossword puzzle:

Across
4 How do you .... 'Bonjour' into English?
6 *happy* and *sad*
8 *in, on, with,* etc.
9 a smile or a frown
10 *find out* and *go away* are .... verbs
11 *the* and *a*

Down
1 *thumbs-up* and *OK*
2 *in a good mood* or *in a bad temper*
3 *go* and *come*
5 *b, c, d, f,* etc.
6 *happily* and *well*
7 *a, e, i, o, u*

3 There are 20 words connected with money, shopping and clothes in this puzzle. Can you find them all?

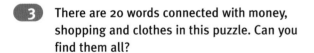

```
i a o g n p c r e d i t c a r d p s
y l c a s h d e s k g a m e y o z h
i l p s s d s s a l a r y d g p i o
s o p h i d o l l a r a n o y o p p
l w s t r e e t m a r k e t h u p p
e a s y p p y c o u n t e r n e i
e n c e g g s h i r t a o a a d c n
v c a p o c k e t m o n e y h n h g
e e r s a n d a l s s s e u r o a m
d o f g e n a n e p c u f f s y n a
d d a o o s u p e r m a r k e t g l
i s e p b u t t o n s a y p p s e l
```

Grammar review

The numbers (1–5) show the unit where the grammar points were first introduced.

A Fill each gap with a suitable word or phrase:

1 I usually ......*do*...... my homework on Sunday evening. But last Sunday
   I ....n't .... my homework, I .... to the cinema instead. And I still
   ....n't .... my homework, sorry!

2 Tom's little sister only goes .... school .... the morning. .... lunch
   .... her aunt, she spends the afternoon .... her grandmother before her
   mother gets home .... work .... six o'clock .... the evening.

3 At .... weekend in .... summer .... older members of my family
   enjoy playing .... game of cards in .... house, but .... younger ones
   prefer to stay out in .... garden and have .... chat. In .... winter we
   often sit together around .... same big table for .... whole evening.

4 '............... you .... Susan's parents?'
   'I............... her mother last year, but I ....n't .... her father yet.'

5 On a plane, passengers .... sit in their designated seats – they .... just sit
   anywhere they like. Before take-off they .... do up their seat belts, and they ....
   stand up until the seat belt sign is no longer illuminated. After that they .... leave their
   seats – but they .... run around the plane.

B Rewrite the sentences, using the words in red:

1 The ice turned into water as we heated it.   until
   We heated the ice ....

2 I didn't meet Bill's parents until Sunday.   first
   I met Bill's parents .... time on Sunday.

3 What was the departure time of the plane?   take
   When .... off?

4 It isn't nice to laugh at people.   fun
   You .... of people.

Vocabulary development and pronunciation

Write your answers to these questions:

1 Write these numbers in words:
   £144 ....   8.8 ....
   3¾ ....   77 km ....

2 Use a dictionary to find 'simple' words you can use instead of these 'harder' words:
   matrimony ....   kin ....   authoritarian ....
   retail outlet ....   remuneration ....

3 Match the words in red to the ones in blue that rhyme:

   bought   feel   gone   hill   money   one   said   through

   fill   funny   head   John   seal   taught   blue   won

4 Write a word that fits with each phrase:
   Can I .... a suggestion?   Could you .... me a favour?
   She .... her homework without .... any mistakes.

5 Add prefixes to these adjectives, to make their opposites:
   ......*un*...happy   ....possible   ....visible   ....convenient
   ....expensive   ....necessary   ....clear   ....likely

6A The best holiday ever!

A great holiday

Speaking and vocabulary

1 👥 **Look at the photos and discuss these questions:**

- What kind of holiday do you like best?
- What do you like to do on holiday?
- What do you do during your summer holidays?

👥👥 **Match these words to the kind of holiday shown in each photo:**

backpack/rucksack   book   camera   fun   guide-book   phrase-book   sandals
seafood   sightseeing   city tour   souvenirs   sun-bed   sun cream   sunglasses
suntan   swimsuit   towel   walking shoes   water-sports

2 👥 **Fill each gap with a suitable word or phrase from below:**

1   Although I *checked in* .... for my .... two hours early, hoping to get a nice window ...., I could only get an .... seat. So I couldn't look out as we .... After we .... I had to wait an hour at ...., then another half hour for my .... I didn't get to my .... in the city till after midnight.

2   In a hotel you can pay for your room only, or for bed and .... (B&B), or you can pay for .... (dinner, bed and breakfast) or .... (all meals). It's much cheaper to rent a .... apartment and do your own cooking. Some resorts are .... – you don't even pay for drinks.

3   We stayed in a luxurious .... hotel: I had a small .... room .... the car park, while my parents had a .... with a big double bed, ... and a .... with a wonderful .... of the mountains. It wasn't fair!

accommodation   air-conditioning   aisle   all-inclusive   balcony   breakfast
~~checked in~~   five-star   flight   full-board   half-board   landed   luggage/suitcase
overlooking   passport control   seat   self-catering   single   suite   took off   view

3 👥👥 **Discuss these questions:**

- What was your best holiday? Why was it good?
- If you could go anywhere in the world on holiday . . .
  . . . where would you go, and why?
  . . . who would you go with, and why?

Travel and holidays

30

The future

1 First look at the examples in the Grammar reference section on pages 122 and 123. Then
Highlight the verbs in this conversation – they all refer to the future:

> *One of these days, if I have enough money, I'm going to fly to New York. I'll*
> *probably stay with my uncle while I'm there.*
> *— Oh, I'm flying there today on business. My plane takes off at noon.*
> *Will you get to the airport on time?*
> *— Oh, I'll take a taxi. It will only take half an hour.*
> *What if the traffic is bad?*

2 Fill the gaps in these sentences using the verbs on the right:

1 What .... *are* .... you .... *doing / going to do* .... next weekend?
2 Do you think the weather .... fine tomorrow?
3 I won't go out until it .... raining.
4 If you're feeling cold I .... the window.
5 When .... the next train to London .... ?
6 When .... you .... your room?
7 The film .... at 7.30, so don't be late!
8 I'm nervous because I .... the dentist this afternoon.

be
close
leave
see
start
stop
tidy

3 👥👥 **Ask each other these questions:**

* What are you going to do next weekend?
* What are your plans for this evening?
* What about your next holiday? What are you going to do?

Vowels – 2: diphthongs

1 🔊 **Listen to the recording and say these words aloud:**

eɪ plane · late   əʊ nose · joke   aɪ time · climb   aʊ round · house
ɔɪ join · choice   ɪə hear · serious   eə hair · care

2 🔊 **Listen to the recording and write down the words you hear:**

1 *shape*	5	9	13 ....
2	6	10	14 ....
3	7	11	15 ....
4	8	12	16 ....

Look at **Activity 45** to see the correct answers. Then say all the words aloud:

3 🔊 **Listen to the recording and fill the gaps with the words you hear. Then take turns to read
the complete sentences aloud.**

1 eɪ   We all had to .... for .... for Jane and that made us .... for the
play. I .... being late.
2 ɪə   It's December: we're .... at the end of the ....
3 əʊ   No-one .... what's going to happen .... – until Tony ....!
4 aɪ   I tried to .... a ticket for a daytime ...., but the price was
too ...., so I decided to fly at ....
5 aʊ   'How do I get to the .... centre?'
'Go .... the next .... and then .... the hill.'
6 ɔɪ   Don't .... the boys' .... while they're playing with their ....
7 eə   'Where's Claire? Is she ....?' 'She's .... washing her ....'

6B Travelling abroad

Dos and don'ts

1 👥 **Look at the photo and discuss these questions:**

- What's happening in the photo?
- When do people in your country salute the national flag?
- When is the national anthem played? Do you know all the words?
- How patriotic are people in your country?

2 👥 **Read this text and then answer the questions below:**

Visiting the USA: Dos & Don'ts

The USA is a very well-ordered society and, generally speaking, people stand in line, obey the rules and follow the instructions. You should be punctual for any business or social occasion and be appropriately dressed.

1

Both men and women shake hands. Family and friends may hug and kiss each other. It's usually OK to use first names. Police and other officials call people 'Sir' and 'Ma'am' and prefer to be addressed as 'Officer'.

2

Self-confidence and a positive outlook are highly valued in the USA, so if someone asks, 'How are you?' the correct answer is 'Fine, thanks,' 'Very well' or something even better. 'Have a nice day' is a common way of saying goodbye and it's also common to say 'You're welcome' after being thanked.

3

The level of patriotism in the USA is very high, and the visitor should remember this. The national flag, known as 'The Stars and Stripes' or 'Old Glory', flies over every school, library and government office, outside many businesses and in front of many private houses. It's more than a symbol – American schoolchildren swear allegiance to the flag every morning and are taught to never let it touch the ground.

4

The national anthem is played at public occasions, such as sports events. Everyone stands and many people place a hand on their heart. People in uniform salute, while civilian men remove their hats (this may be the only time some baseball caps are removed). Most people join in the singing.

5

Underneath all this is a very real sense of national pride, and you should be aware of it when discussing political and social issues. Freedom of speech is one thing, but critical comments about America, especially from a foreigner, can provoke a very negative reaction.

6

Some other don'ts for foreign visitors are:
- Don't assume that Americans know anything about your country, or even where it is.
- Don't smoke anywhere unless smoking is clearly permitted.
- Don't discard any litter, except in a bin.
- Don't forget to tip your waiter or waitress 15% to 20% in restaurants.

7

3 👥 **Which of these statements are true or false, according to the text?**
1. In the USA you should arrive a few minutes late for an appointment.
2. You should address a male police officer as 'Sir'.
3. Americans don't like people to be too modest or pessimistic.
4. You should not criticize American politics.
5. Most Americans know a lot about other countries.
6. Smoking is not allowed in many public places.

4 👥 Highlight the words or phrases in the text which mean the same as these words or phrases. (¶1 = 1st paragraph)

¶1 queue up   follow   on time
¶2 put their arms around each other
¶3 an optimistic attitude
¶5 official or military clothes   non-military
¶6 unfavourable   cause
¶7 throw away   give extra money for good service

5 👥 Which of the advice in the text could be helpful for a first-time visitor to your country? Which would be untrue or unhelpful?

6 ✎ Write your advice for American visitors to your own country, in the same style as the text.

Here are some useful phrases:

You should . . .   *You shouldn't . . .*
It's a good idea to . . .   *It's not a good idea to . . .*
People will expect you to . . .   *People will be upset if you . . .*

Tourist attractions   Speaking

1 👥 Note down the names of FIVE places you think a friend from abroad should visit in your city or region. Discuss these questions about each place:

• What does the place look like? How do you get there?
• Why is the place popular with tourists?
• Have you been there? What did you enjoy about it? Would you like to go there again with your friend?

. . . is very interesting because . . .   *My friend would like . . . because . . .*
Another place to visit is . . .   *I don't think . . . is worth visiting.*

2 👥 One of you should look at Activity 4 on page 132, the other at Activity 24 on page 137. You'll find out more about some riverside tourist attractions in London.

🌐 Find out more @
www.tate.org.uk/modern +
www.towerbridge.org.uk

Travel and holidays

33

7A Home, sweet home

Where do you live?

1 👥 **Look at the two rooms and discuss these questions:**

* Which room do you prefer, and why?
* Which person is more like you?
* How is your home different from the ones in the photos?

2 👥 **Match the words to the pictures:**

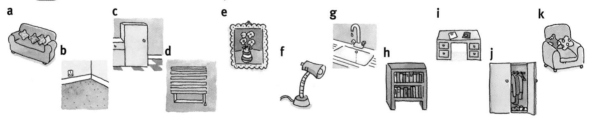

armchair   blind   bookcase   carpet   cupboard   desk
painting   reading lamp   sink   sofa   wardrobe

3 👥 Draw a floor-plan of your own homes, including your own room. Write the names of the furniture and equipment in each room. Use a dictionary, if necessary.

4 👥 + 👥 Join another pair and find out about each other's homes.

Wh– questions

1 First look at the examples in the Grammar reference section on page 123.

2 Complete the questions on the right:

1	She opened the door.	– Why	_did she open the door_ ?
2	He fell asleep in the bath.	– Why	......................?
3	They ate all the cakes.	– Why	......................?
4	Someone broke the window.	– Who	......................?
5	They moved to another town.	– Which	......................?
6	Their house has lots of rooms.	– How	......................?

3 Here are the answers – what were the questions?

1 How ...... *many people live in your* .... apartment?
   – There are four of us: me, my sister and my parents.

2 Who .... family?
   – My grandmother. She's eighty-two.

3 Where .... live?
   – My grandmother? She still lives in a village in the country.

4 How .... to her house?
   – From where we live it takes about three hours by car.

5 How .... her village?
   – We go there a couple of times a year.

6 When .... next?
   – Probably at Easter. Or she may come to visit us.

4 Rewrite these questions as more polite indirect questions:

1 Why is the sky blue?   – Can you tell me ...... *why the sky is blue* .... ?
2 When does the train arrive?   – Do you know .... ?
3 How old are you?   – May I ask .... ?
4 Where is the toilet?   – Could you tell me .... ?
5 How long does the film last? – Does anyone know .... ?
6 How can I get to town from here? – Please tell me ....

Intonation – 1

1 🔊 Listen to the recording, then read the sentences aloud to yourself:

> *Statements usually fall at the end of a sentence.*
> —*You mean like this?*
> *No, like this. But if a sentence is not finished, like this, the voice rises a little, before falling at the end.*
> —*Do Yes/No questions usually rise?*
> *Yes they do.*
> —*And statements that are questions?*
> *Yes, they rise too.*
> —*How about Wh- questions?*
> *They usually fall at the end.*
> —*Is that all I need to know?*
> *Yes, for the time being. But you may need to practise.*

👁 Not everyone speaks the same. Rising and falling intonation varies from speaker to speaker.

2 🔊 Listen to the recording and decide if the end of each line rises ↗ or falls ↘ at the end.

3 👥 Then role play the conversation, or improvise a conversation about your own home.

WHAT DID WE DO BEFORE WIDESCREEN TV?

> *Where do you live?* .... ↘
> —*We used to live in an apartment,* .... ↗
> *but now we live in a house.* ....
> *What kind of house do you live in?* ....
> —*It has three bedrooms.* ....
> *Do you have your own bedroom?* ....
> —*No, I share it with my sister.* ....
> *Your younger sister?* ....
> —*No, my twin sister.* ....
> *You have a twin sister?* ....
> —*Yes, didn't you know?* ....
> *No, I had no idea!* ....

Where I live

7B My home town

Where are you from?

Listening

1 🔊 **Listen to the recording. You'll hear three people describing their home town. Fill the gaps in these summaries:**

Mary is from Brighton. Two nice things are: .... and	Tom is from San Diego. Two nice things are: .... and	Brenda is from Melbourne. Two nice things are: .... and ....
One not so nice thing is:	One not so nice thing is:	One not so nice thing is: ....
The population is:	The population is:	The population is: ....
The weather in summer is:	The weather in summer is:	The weather in summer is: ....

2 👥 **Discuss these questions:**

- Which of the places sounded the nicest?
- Which sounded the worst? Why?
- Which would you like to visit and why?
- What are the two nicest things and the two worst things about *your* home town?

3 👥 + 👥 **Join another pair and compare your answers to the last question. (If you come from different places, talk about the differences between them.)**

🌐 Find out more @
www.brighton.co.uk +
www.visitmelbourne.com +
www.sandiego.org

Why use questions?

1 In a composition, questions can be used rather like headings. Highlight the questions in the text below.

How do questions like these make a text easier to read?

> Motorists in London have to pay to enter the central zone during the daytime.
>
> What are the advantages of this scheme?
>
> First, the charge discourages people from using cars and encourages them to use public transport instead. Why is this a good idea? Well, because there will be fewer cars, there will be less congestion and pollution.
>
> But there are also disadvantages. What are they? First, . . .

2 ✎ In a letter or an e-mail, you can use questions to ask the reader for information:

> How much does a single room cost?
> Do I need to reserve a room?

But a writer can also ask questions to **give** information. This can make the writing seem more friendly and more like a conversation:

> Do you want to know more about me? I expect you do!
> How many people are in my family? Well, there are four of us...
> Where do we live? Well, our flat is quite close to...

Write an e-mail introducing yourself and your home town to a new friend from another country. Use questions to introduce the main points.

Asking and answering questions

1 ◀)) Quite often we need to think for a moment before answering a question. Listen to some useful phrases and practise saying them:

> Why do you like living in a city?
> Why do people live in cities?

> Well, I'm glad you asked me that!
> That's a good question!
> Well, let me think . . .
> Let me see . . .
> I need to think about that for a moment.
> What a difficult question!
> That's easy . . .

2 ✎ Note down FIVE questions beginning with 'Why . . .?'

👥 Join a partner and ask each other questions. Try using the phrases above.

3 👥👥 Discuss these topics, again try using the phrases above:

city life · country life
living in the city centre · living in the suburbs
living in an apartment · living in a house
living with your family · living alone

8A At the movies

What kinds of films do you like?

1 👥 **Look at the pictures and discuss these questions:**

- How many *Lord of the Rings* and *Harry Potter* films have you seen? Which did you enjoy most – and why?
- How often do you go to the cinema?
- How often do you watch films on TV, DVD or video?
- What kind of films do you enjoy? Arrange these in order of preference:

action	adventure	classic	comedy	documentary	drama	fantasy

horror   martial arts   romance   sci-fi   western

2 👥 **Here are some words to describe films. Which are positive and which are negative?**

really
very
quite
too

clever   disappointing   dull   enjoyable   exciting
funny   long   romantic   sad   sentimental   silly
strange   violent   worth seeing

3 👥 **Note down the titles of 4 films you've both seen. Then fill in this chart with your opinions:**

🌐 Find out more @
www.harrypotter.com
+ lordoftherings.net

For reviews of
current films:
empireonline.co.uk +
www.premiere.com +
movie-review.
colossus.net

film title	good points	bad points	verdict
1			
2			
3			
4			

4 👥 + 👥 **Join another pair and compare your charts. Then discuss these questions:**

- Which do you prefer: an English-language film in its original version with subtitles, or dubbed into your language? Why?
- Which do you prefer: a happy ending or a realistic ending? Why?

Reported speech

1 First look at the examples in the Grammar reference section on pages 123 and 124.

2 👥 Read the reports and write what the characters actually said:

1 Brody said they were going to need a bigger boat.
'You're going to need a bigger boat'

2 Jack shouted that he was the king of the world.

3 Darth Vader told Luke he was his father.

4 The Terminator said he would be back.

5 Glinda asked Dorothy if she was a good witch or a bad witch.
Dorothy said she wasn't a witch at all. She was Dorothy, from Kansas.

6 Rick told Louis he thought it was the beginning of a beautiful friendship.

7 Gandalf told Frodo he had to remember that the Ring was trying to get back to its master. It wanted to be found.

3 👥 Read what these characters actually said, and rewrite each sentence in reported speech:

1 'There's no place like home.' — Dorothy said that *there was no place like home* .

2 'I'll make him an offer he can't refuse.' — Don Vito said that he ....

3 'Major Strasser has been shot.' — The police chief said that ....
'Round up the usual suspects.' — He told his men ....

4 'I am a Jedi like my father before me.' — Luke said that ....

5 'We'll always have Paris.' — Rick told Ilse that ....

6 'Snakes, why did it have to be snakes?' — Indiana Jones asked why ....

7 'After all, tomorrow is another day.' — Scarlett O'Hara said that ....

Opposites

1 👥 Match the words in red to their opposites in green:

boring	long	cheap	short
bright	narrow	dark/dull	simple
cloudy	sad	fast/quick	straight
complicated	silly	happy	strong
cool	slow	intelligent	sunny
curved	strange	interesting	tiny
expensive	stupid	normal	warm
huge	weak	sensible	wide

2 👥 Fill the gaps in these sentences:

1 The film wasn't long, it was ....

2 The bags weren't light, they were ....

3 The coffee wasn't weak, it was ....

4 The instructions weren't complicated, they were ....

5 Most film stars aren't ugly, they're ....

6 A cinema seat isn't cheap, it's ....

7 It doesn't take me a long time to get home, it takes ....

8 It's not going to be warm tomorrow, it's going to be.................. .

'Is it any good?'

8B That's show business!

Resonance fm

1 🔊 👥 Listen to a clip from a radio programme. What is your reaction to it?

2 👥 The paragraphs in this article (**A** to **F**) are in the wrong order. Rearrange them in the correct order.

1 .... 2 .... 3 .... 4 .... 5 .... 6 ....

Resonance 104.4 fm – the art of listening

Caroline Kraabel, with Clement, broadcasting live into her mobile phone.

A 'Reverso Mondo doesn't record his voice backwards. He actually talks like that,' says Knut Aufermann, programme manager of the London-based station. 'He has trained himself to speak backwards.'

B Kraabel's idea for the show came when she had a baby and could no longer practise her instrument regularly. 'Art is created out of finding solutions to everyday problems,' says Kraabel, a long-term member of the LMC. 'Clement is demanding, but he is quiet when we go out and he loves me playing, so it works well. What I play is quite simple because I can only use my left hand. Occasionally Clement sings as well, which is great, but mostly he falls asleep.'

C One of the most interesting, and strangely charming shows on the station is Taking a Life for a Walk, on which musician Caroline Kraabel walks around the streets near her London home, pushing her 18-month-old son Clement with one hand and holding a saxophone with the other. As she goes about her daily business – visiting the post office, taking Clement to the swings – she improvises with her environment on the sax and the music is broadcast live from the mobile phone attached to her head.

D Resonance fm grew out of the London Musician's Collective, a non-profit organization set up to support the growth of live, experimental music. Everyone works for free. There is no advertising, so the station is dependent on grants.

E 'We want to give an outlet to things that are not heard elsewhere. There are so many artists who never have the chance to get their work on air.'

F There is a man on the radio who is playing a record backwards. When sound comes to an end, he introduces the track he has just played in a voice that sounds as if it was recorded backwards, placing the emphasis on all the wrong syllables. The man is Reverso Mondo, and absolutely everything about his show is the wrong way round. Repeats come earlier in the week than the original airings, and the first show ever broadcast was of course the last, when he said his goodbyes. It is all part of Resonance fm, the strangest radio station in Britain.

Will Hodgkinson

3 👥 Decide if these summaries of each paragraph are true or false:

¶ A   Reverso Mondo has learnt to talk backwards.
¶ B   Clement doesn't enjoy his mother's music.
¶ C   Caroline composes her music when Clement is asleep.

🌐 Find out more @
www.resonance.fm.com

Resonance104.4**fm**
the art of listening

¶ D   None of Resonance fm's artists is paid.
¶ E   Many of Resonance fm's artists also broadcast on other stations.
¶ F   Reverso Mondo's last programme was broadcast first.

4 **Discuss these questions:**

- If you had your own radio station, what would you broadcast?
- Which are your favourite radio stations, and why?
- Which are your favourite TV programmes, and why?

Your review   Writing

1 **Read these reviews, then discuss the questions below:**

'The Two Towers' is the second in the "Lord Of The Rings" trilogy. It was violent from beginning to end. There were non-stop battles and fighting, all totally unbelievable because the evil characters were all computer-generated. There were a few funny moments, but not enough. The three different stories were very confusing.

The film was extremely long and the DVD version was even longer than the one shown in cinemas.

All in all, I found the film disappointing and I was glad when it had finished.

Verdict: Not worth seeing.

'The Two Towers' was a wonderful film, full of excitement and humour. The Gollum character was amazing – he was both horrible and funny. He spoke terrible English! 'We wants it, we needs it. Must have the precious.'

The battle scenes were thrilling, with thousands of evil creatures attacking the good men and elves.

The music was brilliant too. The DVD includes many scenes which weren't shown in the cinema version and interesting interviews with the director and actors.

Verdict: Highly recommended.

- Which review do you prefer – and why?
- Do you read film reviews? Why/Why not?
- Who are your favourite stars?
- If one of your favourite stars is in a movie, do you always go to see it?

2 **Write a review of a film you have seen.**

Encouraging the other speaker   Speaking

1 **Listen to the conversation and tick the phrases that the speakers use:**

| Are you with me? | Do you see what I mean? | OK? |
| Am I being clear? | Right? | You see? |

I see.	Oh really?	That's interesting.	OK.
Go on.	Right.	Sure.	Cool.
Uh-huh.	Mm-hm.	Absolutely.	

2 **Practise saying the phrases.**

3 One of you should look at Activity 5 on page 132, the other at Activity 25 on page 138. Use your own words to tell the story of the movie, using the phrases above.

4 Tell your partners the story of a film you have seen recently. Encourage each other.

9A What do you mean?

Faces and voices

1  2  3  4  5

1 👥 Look at the pictures and match the faces to the feelings by filling in the chart below:

emotion	face number	voice number	verb or noun
angry			
bored			
happy			
terrified			
interested			
puzzled			
sad			
surprised			
disappointed			

2 🔊 Listen to the recording and decide what feeling each person is showing. Write the number in the chart above.

3 👥 Compare your answers, then add these verbs and nouns to the last column in the chart:

cry   tears   frown   gasp   glare
laugh   scream   sigh   smile   yawn

4 👥👥 Discuss these questions:

- Why was it sometimes difficult to hear what feelings the people were showing?
- Which feelings were hardest to recognize?
- If somebody frowns they may be puzzled – but what else can a frown mean?
  Or if someone sighs? Or if they smile?

'Pay no attention to me. I'll be just fine.'

–ing and *to* . . . – 1

1 First look at the examples in the Grammar reference section on page 124.

2 Select a suitable verb from the box and then fill each gap with a suitable form:

1 Have you ever thought of ....*learning*........... Russian?
2 It was difficult .... what she was saying.
3 I was afraid .... the phone in case it was bad news.
4 I enjoy .... but I don't like .... afterwards.
5 If I'm not here, please ask him .... a message.
6 .... a text message is cheaper than phoning.
7 I was happy .... that she had passed her test.
8 Are you interested in .... to the cinema with me tonight?

answer
come
cook
hear
learn
leave
send
understand
wash up

3 Write a complete sentence for each prompt below, using these patterns:

It's easier to . . . than to . . .	*–ing* is easier than *–ing*
It's easier to read a book than to write one.	*Reading a book is easier than writing one.*
It's more fun to . . .	*–ing* is more fun than . . .
It takes longer to . . .	*–ing* takes longer than . . .
It's quicker to . . .	*–ing* is quicker than . . .
It's cheaper to . . .	*–ing* is cheaper than . . .
It's better to . . .	*–ing* is better than . . .

1 learn   Italian   Japanese
2 talk to   friends   strangers

It's easier to talk to friends than talk to strangers.

3 listen to   pop music   classical music
4 play   basketball   golf
5 fly to   London   New York
6 walk to   school   the city centre
7 send   an e-mail   a letter
8 go to   the cinema   the opera
9 go   bike   car

Collocations – 2

Vocabulary development

1 Match the verbs in red with the words in blue:

answer	make	a letter	an e-mail
dial	open	a message	an envelope
leave	send	a number	the phone
lift	write	a phone call	the receiver

2 Guess what word comes next in each of these sentences:

1 As it's her birthday next week I'm going to send her a ....
2 We went into the city by ....
3 When I told him the bad news he was very ....
4 What time does the film .... ?
5 How much did your new shoes .... ?
6 How long does the journey from here to London .... ?
7 How long does 'The Lord of the Rings' .... ?
8 What is the answer to this .... ?

👥 + 👥 **Compare your answers. Explain why you chose different words.**

Communication

Put it in writing

The man who invented e-mail

1 👥 Read this article and then answer the questions below:

Ray Tomlinson is the man who invented e-mail. Back in 1971 he was working in a team of programmers who were working on a program called SNDMSG ('send message') that allowed users of the same computer to leave messages for one another – a sort of single-computer version of an e-mail system. They were working on the ARPANET, which was set up by the US Defense Department's Advanced Research Projects Agency to connect different research computers, and which later developed into the Internet.

Ray wanted to distinguish between messages that were headed out onto the network and those that were addressed to users in the same office. He studied the keyboard for a symbol that didn't occur naturally in people's names and that wasn't a digit. He chose the @ symbol to indicate that the user was 'at' some other distant host rather than being local – and @ is the only preposition on the keyboard.

Before this, the purpose of the @ sign (in English) was to indicate a unit price (for example, 10 items @ $1.95). At the time Ray says he gave it only '30 to 40 seconds of thought'.

To test the program he sent a message to another computer. The message was something quite forgettable, and he has now forgotten what it was. Electronic mail is now known as e-mail or email. Domain names (apple.com, cambridge.org, etc.) were not used until 1984. Before that each host was only known by its IP (Internet protocol) address number.

Ray's ideas changed the world and made a lot of others rich, but not him. 'Innovation is sometimes rewarded,' he says modestly, 'but not this innovation!'

Note down your answers to these questions:

1 When did Ray invent e-mail?
2 What does the abbreviation 'ARPA' in ARPANET stand for?
3 What did the symbol @ mean before Ray started using it?
4 How long did it take Ray to decide to use @?
5 What was Ray's first message?
6 How much money did Ray make?

 Find out more @ www.bbn.com

2 👥 Fill in this chart about yourselves, then discuss the questions below:

In an average week, how many times do you ...					
	you	partner		you	partner
write an e-mail?			receive an e-mail?		
write a letter?			receive a letter?		
write a greetings card?			receive a greetings card?		
write a postcard?			receive a postcard?		
make a phone call?			receive a phone call?		

- Which methods do you prefer, and why?
- Are there any methods you never or hardly ever use? Why?
- On your birthday (or name day) which do you prefer to receive, and why?

Exciting writing!!

In speech your voice can make a word like 'nice' or 'good' sound exciting.

In writing you can use <u>underlining</u> or CAPITALS or **bold print** or *italics* or colour – or an exclamation mark! But a more forceful word may be better.

1 👥 Look at the words and phrases in the lists below. Which ones are only normally used about food? Highlight the words you want to remember.

The meal was <u>good</u>.   Tests are <u>bad</u>.   I <u>like</u> chocolate.   I <u>dislike</u> tests.
The meal was <u>nice</u>.

amazing	lovely	appalling	adore	can't stand
brilliant	marvellous	awful	am keen on	can't bear
delicious	superb	disgusting	am mad about	detest
excellent	tasty	dreadful	love	hate
fantastic	terrific	horrible		loathe
great	wonderful	terrible		

2 👥 Find a more exciting word or phrase you can use in place of the grey words in each sentence.

1 It was nice weather so we decided to go for a bike ride.
2 It was a good party. Thank you for inviting me.
3 I like going to the cinema.
4 I thought it was a bad film.
5 You're going on holiday? Have a nice time!
6 We had a good meal.
7 I don't like doing homework.
8 Thank you for your nice e-mail.

Hesitating and holding the floor

1 🔊 Listen to two conversations. Which conversation goes better and why?

2 🔊 Practise saying these phrases:

> ... um ...
> ... er ...
> Well ...
> ... you see ...
> ... you know ...
> ... and ...

> *Just a moment ...*
> *Hold on ...*
> *One more thing I want to say ...*
> *Let me just finish ...*
> *There's one more thing ...*
> *Oh, and another thing ...*

3 👥 One of you should look at Activity 6 on page 132, the other at Activity 26 on page 138. You'll have a story to tell your partner.

4 ✎ Write your version of one of the stories from either Activity 6 or Activity 26.

EEEEEEEEE-mail

Communication

Different kinds of food

Eating, drinking and cooking

Speaking and vocabulary

1 How many different kinds of fruit and vegetables can you identify in the picture? Ask each other these questions:

- What do you usually have for breakfast? For lunch? Before bed?
- What is your favourite meal of the day? Why?

2 Do this task together. Use a dictionary to help you.

1 Add one more herb and one more spice:

mint   basil   oregano   ....
pepper   paprika   cinnamon   ....

2 Add two more kinds of fish or seafood:

trout   shrimp   lobster   ....

3 Add three more kinds of meat:

chicken   pork   ....

4 Add four more drinks. Then number them in order of preference (1 to 8):

mineral water   iced tea   milkshake   coffee   ....

5 Add five more vegetables. Then number them in order of preference (1 to 7):

carrot   potato   ....

6 Add six more fruits. Then number them in order of preference (1 to 8):

banana   pineapple   ....

3 Match these words to the pictures. Which words are NOT shown in the pictures?

bowl/dish   chopsticks   cup   fork   frying pan   glass   knife   menu
mug   napkin   oven   plate   sandwich   saucepan   saucer   spoon

Comparing

1 First look at the examples in the Grammar reference section on page 125.

2 👥 Look at these sentences. Only two are true – rewrite the untrue statements.

1 Coca-Cola is not as sweet as orange juice.
   That's not true. Coca-Cola is sweeter than orange juice.
2 The water in a river is not safe enough to drink.
3 Sunflower oil is more expensive than olive oil.
4 Ice cream contains less sugar than fresh fruit.
5 Cream does not contain as much fat as milk.
6 Margarine tastes the same as butter.
7 Carrots and oranges are different colours.
8 Water is the cheapest drink there is.

3 Fill the gaps in these sentences:

1 Apple juice is ...*not as*... sweet ......*as*...... honey.
2 Tea doesn't .... bitter .... coffee.
3 Orange juice is .... sour .... lemon juice.
4 Lobster is .... expensive .... salmon.
5 French fries are .... unhealthy .... boiled potatoes.
6 Eating salad is .... healthy .... eating vegetables.
7 Diet lemonade isn't .... bad for you .... normal lemonade.
8 Butter is .... salty .... cheese.

Consonants

1 👥 Take it in turns to read out each letter on this English keyboard:

2 👥 Spell out your own full name letter by letter. Your partner should write it down.
Then, secretly, write down the full names of two famous people.
Spell out each name to your partner letter by letter.

3 🔊 👥 Guess the missing words in each sentence, then listen to the recording to see if you guessed right. Then say the sentences yourself.

1 ...*Lamb*... is the kind of meat we get from ....
2 Do you have fresh orange .... for .... ?
3 Give the .... a good .... when you pay the bill.
4 Can I have a .... slice of bread, not a .... one?
5 When I eat .... it hurts my bad ....
6 .... and .... are both made from milk.
7 .... is an alcoholic drink made from ....
8 When you follow a .... , do you .... the ingredients?

4 👥 Write and say three more words to include these letters:

chip   show   jam   phone   thin   tough

Enjoy your meal!

Eating out

1 👥 **Look at the photos and ask each other these questions:**

- Which place do you prefer – and why?
- What did you have for your last meal? What did you drink? Did you enjoy the meal?

2 🔊 **Anna, Bill and Carole are talking about a meal they remember well. First, decide which of the places above they are describing.**

3 🔊 **Listen again and write the missing information in this chart:**

	Anna	**Bill**	**Carole**
Where?			
When?			
Who with?			
What did you eat?			
Why was it memorable?			

4 👥 **Ask each other these questions:**

- What did you eat the last time you ate out? What did you drink? Did you enjoy your meal?
- What was the best meal you've had this year? (Where? When? Who with? What did you eat? Why was it memorable?)

How to make . . .

1 👥 **Find out about each other's favourite dishes:**

> *What are your favourite . . . ?*
> *What kinds of . . . do you like?*

> —*The . . . I like best is . . .*
> —*I like . . . very much. What about you?*

Write the names of two of your personal favourites in the chart opposite.

'I have some bad news. You've got a nut allergy.'

MY FAVOURITE DISHES				
starters	1	desserts	1	
	2		2	
main courses	1	snacks	1	
	2		2	

✎ Maybe some of the favourites you chose are local dishes, which a foreign person might not know about. Write one sentence in English to explain each one.

2 👥 Read this recipe. Would you use as much cream as the recipe says? Guess the meanings of these words (don't use a dictionary):

bake   short-grain   grate   shallow   sprinkle   dot   topping

Baked rice pudding

SERVES 4–6

100 g short-grain rice
450 ml milk
450 ml cream*
50 g sugar
25 g unsalted butter
freshly grated nutmeg

Pre-heat the oven to 180°C and butter a shallow ovenproof dish. Wash the rice and place in the prepared dish. Heat through the milk and cream in the same saucepan and pour over the rice. Sprinkle the sugar over the rice and mix in. Dot with the butter and grate fresh nutmeg over the top. Bake the pudding for 10 minutes. Then reduce the temperature to 150°C and bake for 1 hour 30 minutes. The pudding should now have a golden brown topping, with rich creamy rice pudding underneath. Serve hot.

* Use less cream and more milk if you wish. Alternatively, use only milk.

3 🔊 Listen to Claire telling Simon how to make baked rice pudding. Which of these phrases does she use?

It's quite easy to prepare.	*Then you . . .*
I'll explain how to prepare it.	*After that you . . .*
First of all . . .	*And finally . . .*
Make sure you . . .	*I hope you enjoy it!*

4 👥 Think of a (simple) dish that you both like. Discuss what ingredients you need and how to prepare the dish.

5 👥 + 👥 Join another pair. Tell each other how to prepare your dishes. Which sounds more delicious? Which sounds easier to prepare?

6 ✎ Write your own recipe. Use the same style as the recipe above.

🌐 Find out more @
www.bbc.co.uk/food

Food and drink

6-10 Revision

Topic vocabulary

7-9 Try this crossword puzzle:

Across
2 A place to keep your clothes
4 A place to keep books
6 More exciting than 'dislike'
10 This expression shows you are cross, or puzzled
11 A foreign-language film can be ....
13 Very bad
14 These come out of your eyes when you cry

Down
1 These keep out the sunlight
3 More exciting than 'like'
5 More exciting than 'good'
7 You may do this if you're terrified!
8 Romantic and silly
9 You can keep things in this piece of furniture
12 An angry look

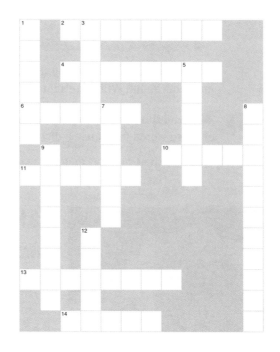

10 There are 25 things you can eat in this puzzle. Can you find them all?

```
b v a r u t s a l t f r e d p e p p e r
s p r i n g o n i o n u e i e a v g t t
l t t e b s s t o m a t o g t f e f s u
f i e b p i n e a p p l e p a b g t b a
v a r a s p b e r r y b c a i r r t e u
r t g p e a r e u v g e i p r o l f e b
i g r e e n b e a n c u n r s c u i f e
i u p a r s l e y e a k n i t c t u c r
r g l o b s t e r l r b a k l o s v r g
s e o r a n g e i o r i m a e l t l r i
g e t v l l l a p l o a o f m i n t t n
b l a c k b e r r y t i n o n i o n r e
l e t t u c e e e b t i l e m o n t e e
s e s e t s l a m b s t r a w b e r r y
```

Grammar review

A Fill each gap with a suitable word or phrase:

6 When I ..... *go* .... on holiday next summer, I .... to either America or Australia, If I .... to America, I .... the Grand Canyon. If I .... to Australia, I .... diving on the Great Barrier Reef. Wherever I ...., I .... have to save up a lot of money.

7 If you go to Australia, when ....? How much .... to get there? How long .... spend there? Who .... with? Where .... last summer holiday? How long .... spend there? Why .... go back to the same place?

The numbers (6–10) show the unit where the grammar points were first introduced.

8 He told me .... to Australia for his holiday. He said the air fare

.... very expensive, but that he .... a cheaper flight if he

.... up early. He said he .... with his brother and they

.... four weeks touring around.

9 On holiday, it's cheaper .... by bus or coach than .... hire a

car, but .... by car gives you more independence. If you enjoy

.... by bus, it's a good way .... people, but it usually takes

longer .... somewhere by bus.

10 There aren't .... people in Australia .... there are in the USA,

but the countries themselves are about .... size. For Europeans, Australia is

.... to get to .... the USA, and flights to the USA are

.... flights to Australia. Australia has .... visitors from Asia

.... the USA.

B **Rewrite the sentences, using the words in red:**

6 What is the starting time of the movie?   begin
When .... ?

7 What was the name of the person who took the message?   leave
Who .... with?

8 'I really enjoyed myself on holiday last summer,' he said.   good
He said that .... time on holiday.

9 Would you like to go to the cinema tonight?   movie
Are you interested .... tonight?

10 *The Matrix* is more violent than *Harry Potter*.   violence
There isn't .... *Harry Potter* .... *The Matrix*.

Vocabulary development and pronunciation

6 **Match the words in red to the ones in blue that rhyme:**

care   crowd   frowned   fuel   my   noise   stay   quite   time   wait
boys   climb   fly   hair   jewel   late   light   loud   may   sound

7 **Add intonation marks (↘ or ↗) to this dialogue, to show how it would be spoken:**

What time do you usually get up? ....
Yes ...., *on a typical weekday.* ....

And if it's raining? ....

On a weekday? ....
If it's fine ...., *I get up early
and go for a run.* ....
I stay in bed! ....

8 **What are the opposites of these adjectives?**

warm   *cool*   complicated   sensible   wide   intelligent   strong   strange

9 **Fill the gaps with suitable collocations:**

I needed to get in .... with my uncle in Canada. I was going to .... him a letter but

the post would .... too long, so I decided to .... a phone call. I .... the number

and waited a long time for someone to .... But he wasn't at home, so I .... a

message on his answering machine. I should have sent him an .... instead.

10 **Match the words in red to the ones in blue that rhyme:**

age   lamb   laugh   match   push   stamp   their   though   worth
birth   bush   catch   half   jam   lamp   page   there   throw

11A Tools and gadgets

Great ideas!

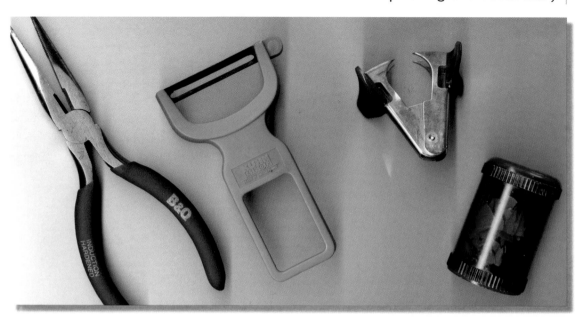

1 Look at the pictures and discuss these questions:

- How do the tools and gadgets in the pictures work, do you think?
- If you didn't have each of them, how would you do the same task?

Write down the names of five more tools or gadgets – use a dictionary if necessary.

2 + Join another pair and compare your lists. Which of the tools and gadgets are most useful to you personally? Why?

3 Can you guess which year each of these inventions were made?

| 1886 | 1938 | 1940 | 1950 | 1965 | 1971 | 1975 | 1976 | 1979 | 1979 | 1990 | 1995 |

| ballpoint pen | CD | colour TV | dishwasher | DVD | e-mail | mobile phone |
| personal computer | remote control | video recorder | Walkman | World Wide Web |

Number them (1 to 12) in order of importance to you personally.
Why is each one important to you? How necessary is it in your life?

The passive

1 First look at the examples in the Grammar reference section on pages 125 and 126.

2 Write the answers to the questions following the same pattern:

1	Who invented television?	*I don't know who it was invented by* .
2	Who discovered X-rays?	I don't know who they ....
3	Who ate the cakes?	I don't know who they ....
4	Who did the washing-up?	I don't know who it ....
5	Who drank all the milk?	I don't know who it ....
6	Who will play the music?	I don't know who it ....

3 👥 Write a question and an answer about each tool, gadget or device:

1 scissors *What are scissors used for* ? *They're used for cutting paper.*
                                              They're used to cut paper.

2 corkscrew *What is a corkscrew used for* ? *It's* .

3 paper clips ....? ....

4 screwdriver ....? ....

5 hammer ....? ....

6 kettle ....? ....

7 alarm clocks ....? ....

8 dictionary ....? ....

What other uses for each thing can you think of, besides the one you wrote down?

Suffixes – 1

Vocabulary development

1 👥 Look at these examples before you do the exercise below:

A suffix can be used to form an adverb from an adjective:

happy · happily   quick · quickly

or a verb from an adjective:

hard · harden

or an adjective from a noun:

wash · washable   help · helpful   season · seasonal   sun · sunny

2 👥 Use suffixes to make adverbs, verbs and adjectives. The words in violet require changes in spelling:

adverbs	**–ly**	funny easy year day hour careful loud particular slight sudden recent equal usual
verbs	**–en**	soft thick fresh loose tight short sweet
adjectives	**–able**	avoid accept enjoy notice prefer understand
	–ful	power hope use
	–al	emotion nature accident nation region department
	–y	cloud fog mud rain snow thirst hunger dirt grass itch hair smoke sun

3 👥 Fill each gap with a suitable adverb, verb or adjective formed from the words above:

1 It was a lovely .... day, so we had a very .... time.

2 A pencil-sharpener is not .... if you always use a ballpoint!

3 I've lost so much weight that I have to .... my belt .... to keep my trousers up!

4 People .... use sugar to .... tea, but she used honey.

5 They spoke so .... that everyone could hear them ....

6 He gets very .... if you mention his former girlfriend and he may even .... begin to cry.

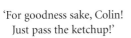

'For goodness sake, Colin!
Just pass the ketchup!'

Science and technology

Why is the sky blue?

Reading

 Can either of you explain why the sky is blue and why snow is white? Or can you guess?

Look at these words – which of them do you already know? Look up the ones you don't know in a dictionary. Then read the two texts.

atoms nitrogen oxygen atmosphere phenomenon scatter particle
transparent translucent photon path layer crystal bounce frequency spectrum

Why is the sky blue?

When you look at the sky at night, it is black, with the stars and the moon forming points of light on that black background. So why is it that, during the day, the sky does not remain black? Why does the daytime sky turn a bright blue and the stars disappear?

The first thing to recognize is that the sun is an extremely bright source of light – much brighter than the moon. The second thing to recognize is that the atoms of nitrogen and oxygen in the atmosphere have an effect on the sunlight that passes through them.

A phenomenon called **Rayleigh scattering** causes light to scatter when it passes through very tiny particles. Sunlight is made up of all different colors of light, but the color blue is scattered much more efficiently than the other colors.

So when you look at the sky on a clear day, you can see the sun as a bright disk. The blueness you see everywhere else is all of the atoms in the atmosphere scattering blue light toward you. And because red light, yellow light, green light and the other colors aren't scattered nearly as well, you see the sky as blue.

Why is snow white?

by Marshall Brain

Since snow is frozen water, and we all know that frozen water is clear, why is snow always white? To understand this, we need to look at an individual piece of ice. Ice is not transparent; it's actually translucent. This means that the light photons don't pass right through the material in a direct path – the material's particles change the light's direction. The light exits the ice in a different direction than it entered the ice.

Snow is a whole bunch of individual ice crystals arranged together. When a light photon enters a layer of snow, it goes through an ice crystal on the top, which changes its direction slightly and sends it on to a new ice crystal, which does the same thing. Basically, all the crystals bounce the light all around so that it comes right back out of the snow. It does the same thing to all the different light frequencies, so all colors of light are bounced back out. The 'color' of all the frequencies in the visible spectrum combined equally is white, so this is the color we see in snow.

 Discuss these questions:

- Which text was more interesting?
- Which scientific facts did you already know?
- What were the two most interesting facts you discovered?
- How interested are you in science? Why?

 Find out more @
www.science.howstuffworks.com

A good start

A good first sentence catches your readers' attention, and shows them what to expect in the following sentences.

1 👥 Compare these sentences with the original first sentences of the texts in Units 6 to 11. Why don't these versions really catch your attention as well as the originals?

Snow is white but frozen water is clear, as we all know.	see page 54
At night the sky is black, in the daytime it is blue.	see page 54
E-mail was invented by a man called Ray Tomlinson.	see page 44
A record is being played backwards on the radio.	see page 40
Most people in the USA stand in line, obey the rules and follow the instructions because it is a very well-ordered society.	see page 32

2 ✏️ 👥 Look at the last three pieces of written work you did. Work together to rewrite the first sentence of each one.

One, two, three

1 🔊 Listen to Emma telling Tony how to programme a video recorder. Put the instructions (A to J) in the correct order (1 to 10):

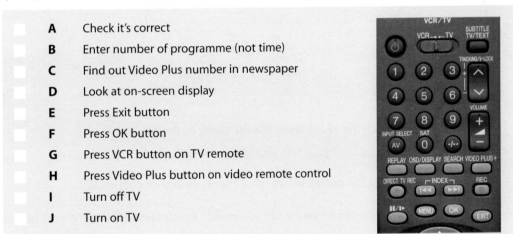

☐	**A**	Check it's correct
☐	**B**	Enter number of programme (not time)
☐	**C**	Find out Video Plus number in newspaper
☐	**D**	Look at on-screen display
☐	**E**	Press Exit button
☐	**F**	Press OK button
☐	**G**	Press VCR button on TV remote
☐	**H**	Press Video Plus button on video remote control
☐	**I**	Turn off TV
☐	**J**	Turn on TV

2 🔊 Practise saying these phrases:

First ...
Then ...
Oh, and before that you have to ...
Don't forget to ...
Remember to ...
And finally ...

First of all ...
After that ...
Oh, but before you do that, you ...
Make sure you ...
It's important to ...
And last of all ...

3 👥 One of you should look at **Activity 8** on page 133, the other at **Activity 29** on page 139. You'll be telling each other how to do something.

Science and technology

Different countries

Where in the world?

1 👥 **Look at the photos and discuss these questions:**

- Can you guess which country is shown in each picture? (See the list below.)
- Which of the countries in the list would you like to visit one day? Why?
- Which have you no wish to visit, and why not?

Australia	Canada	Egypt	Japan	New Zealand
Austria	Chile	England	Mexico	Switzerland
Brazil	China	Greece	Morocco	Thailand

Match the countries in the list above to the continents:

Africa   Asia   Australasia   Europe   North America   South America

Write the names of five more countries in your continent.

2 👥 **Do you know (or can you guess) which category these places belong to?**

Categories	Places	
countries	the Alps	the Mediterranean
states	the Atlantic	Lake Michigan
cities	California	the Nile
counties	Cornwall	the Pacific
oceans	Crete	the Red Sea
lakes	Everest	the Rhine
seas	the Himalayas	Texas
rivers	Holland	Thailand
mountains	Lake Geneva	Venice
mountain ranges	Majorca	Vienna
islands	the Matterhorn	Yorkshire

Add one more example to each category.

Lake Geneva and Lake Michigan are both lakes.
— *I know Everest is a mountain, but I'm not sure about the other one.*
Can you think of another island?

If . . . sentences – 1

1 First look at the examples in the Grammar reference section on page 126.

2 👥 Ask each other what you might do tomorrow, following the pattern on the right:

Activity	Depends on
walk	weather fine
shopping	have enough money
theatre	can get tickets
stay at home	raining
cinema	good film on
work	in the mood
watch TV	nothing else to do

What are you going to do tomorrow?
— I'll go for a walk if the weather is fine.
But what if it isn't fine?
— I certainly won't go for a walk if it isn't fine.

3 👥 Look at the example. Then use the same pattern to make more sentences about the countries in the list.

Holland   If *you lived in Holland, you'd have to speak Dutch.*

Egypt   Brazil   Chile   Taiwan   Poland   Belgium   Switzerland

And what would you be able to **see** or **do** in each country? Think of a more interesting ending for each sentence. For example:

If you lived in Holland, you'd be able to see Amsterdam and visit the Van Gogh Museum.

4 👥 Complete these sentences with your own ideas:

1 If I was English, *I wouldn't need to come to English classes* .
2 If I had lots of money, ...
3 If I was a famous film star, ...
4 If I was the president of my country, ...
5 If I was more confident, ...
6 If I was ten years older than I am, ...
7 If I was ten years younger, ...
8 If I didn't have to go to English classes, ...

Nationalities and adjectives

1 👥 Look at the examples. Then write the adjectives for the other places:

–an   Europe – European   Italy – Italian   Russia – Russian

Africa   America   Asia   Australia   Austria   Belgium   Brazil   Canada   Chile   Egypt
India   Mexico   Morocco

2 👥 Look at the examples. Then write the adjectives for the other places:

–ish   Scotland – Scottish   Ireland – Irish   Cornwall – Cornish   ,

Britain   England   Poland   Spain   Sweden   Turkey

3 👥 Which country do these people come from?

a Welshman   a Chinese person   a Greek   a Dutchwoman   a Japanese person
a Swiss person   a Frenchman   a German   a Czech   a Portuguese person

4 👥 Is your country missing from the lists? Add your country – and also any countries which share a border with your country.

The other side of the world

A different experience

1 👥 **Discuss these questions:**

- What do tourists do if they go to Australia? What can they see there?
- If you went to Australia, what would you do there?

2 🔊 **Listen to Ralph Jackson and Kristi O'Brien talking about their travel companies. Tick the information they give:**

Find out more @
www.waywardbus.com.au +
www.diversetravel.com.au

	Wayward Bus	Diverse Travel Australia
Meet Australian Aboriginal people	☐	☐
Groups of up to 21 people	☐	☐
See Australian animals in the wild	☐	☐
Visit Kangaroo Island	☐	☐
'Hop on hop off' where you like	☐	☐
Trips last one day to one month	☐	☐
Trips last 2 days to 10 days	☐	☐
Drive the Great Ocean Road (Adelaide–Melbourne)	☐	☐
Motto: 'Let the others rush'	☐	☐
Don't visit the usual tourist destinations	☐	☐

3 👥 **Discuss these questions:**

- What would you enjoy about a trip with Wayward Bus or Diverse Travel?
- What would you not enjoy?

Around the world

A good ending

Your final sentence is even more important than your first. A memorable final sentence leaves your readers feeling satisfied with what they have read, and with a good last impression of your work.

1 👥 Compare these sentences with the original final sentences of the texts in Units 6 to 11. Why are these versions less effective than the originals?

The color we see in snow is white because white is the 'color' of all the frequencies in the visible spectrum combined equally.	see page 54
You see the sky as blue because red light, yellow light, green light and the other colors aren't scattered nearly as well as blue is.	see page 54
Serve the pudding hot. It will now have a golden brown topping, and there will be rich creamy rice pudding underneath.	see page 49
He says modestly that although innovation is sometimes rewarded, his innovation was not rewarded.	see page 44
'Clement mostly falls asleep, but sometimes he sings as well.'	see page 40
In spite of freedom of speech, if a foreigner makes critical comments about America, it can provoke a very negative reaction.	see page 32

2 ✎ 👥 Look at the last four pieces of written work you each did. Which is the best of the four? Work together to rewrite the other three.

That's not right!

1 🔊 Tony is talking to Betty, a good friend, and to Mrs Frost, an older acquaintance. Which of the phrases does he say to each person?

	to Betty	to Mrs Frost
Sydney is the capital of Australia.		
A mile is the same as a kilometre.		
New Zealand is bigger than Australia.		

	to Betty	to Mrs Frost
I'm sorry, that's not right.	☐	☐
I don't think that's right.	☐	☐
Are you quite sure about that?	☐	☐
I'm not sure that's right.	☐	☐
I don't think so.	☐	☐
That's completely wrong!	☐	☐
No, you're wrong!	☐	☐
That's nonsense!	☐	☐
Don't be so silly!	☐	☐

2 🔊 Practise saying the phrases in the speech bubble on the right, above.

3 👤 Write down ten UNtrue sentences – as in these examples:

The Atlantic is larger than the Pacific.
Canberra is the capital of Germany

👥 Give each other the false information – and react appropriately!

'She never had children.'

Lovely weather!

What's the weather going to be like?

1 🔊 👥 **Listen to two weather forecasts. Fill in the missing information in the charts, then discuss the questions below:**

SATURDAY	weather	temp
morning		
lunchtime		
afternoon		
evening		
overnight		

SUNDAY	weather	temp
morning		
lunchtime		
afternoon		
evening		
overnight		

- Which day is going to be better? What would you do on each day?
- How does the weather affect your mood and your activities?

2 👥 **Decide together what the difference is between . . .**

snow	and	sleet
rain		drizzle
a hot day		a heatwave
a shower		a downpour
a breeze		a gale
a cloud		fog
frost		ice

*Snow is white and cold,
sleet is a wet sort of snow –
a sort of snowy rain or rainy snow.*

3 👥 + 👥 **Join another pair and compare your explanations. Then discuss these questions:**

- What kinds of weather do you like best of all?
- What kind of weather do you hate?
- What was the weather like last week?
- What do you think the weather is going to be like next week?

🌐 Find out more @ www.weather.com +
www.metoffice.com + www.bbc.co.uk/weather

Reported questions

1 **First look at the examples in the Grammar reference section on page 126 and at the section on reported speech on pages 123 and 124.**

2 🔊 **First, listen to the examples:**

Student A: *What's the weather going to be like tomorrow? Ask Charlie for me.*

Student B: *Alex wants to know what the weather is going to be like tomorrow.*

Student C: *I think it's going to be hot.*

Student B: *Charlie says he thinks it's going to be hot.*

Student A: *OK. Now ask Charlie a question and he'll ask me.*

👤 Secretly, write five questions about
different topics, not only the weather.

👥👤 Sit in a circle. Take turns to
start each exchange. Talk softly
or whisper.

3 👥 Report these questions:

1 'Is it going to be sunny?'   *He asked me if it was going to be sunny* .
2 'Will you be free to come out with us?'   She asked me ....
3 'Have you seen my pen anywhere?'   He asked me ....
4 'Where is my bag?'   She wanted to know ....
5 'Do you want me to look for it?'   I wondered ....
6 'How long will the exercise take?'   She didn't know ....
7 'Why are you sitting in the dark?'   He asked ....

4 👥👥 Rejoin the same group as in 2. Remember the questions and answers you gave and report them, as in this example: *Student A wanted to know what the weather was going to be like, and Student C said it was going to be hot.*

Suffixes – 2: nouns

Vocabulary development

1 👥 Look at these examples before you do the exercise below:

A suffix can be used to name people who do particular things:

swim · swimmer   act · actor   piano · pianist

or to name things with a particular function: can opener   projector

or to form a noun from a verb or adjective:

happy · happiness   punish · punishment   educate · education   perform · performance
generous · generosity   decide · decision   combine · combination   warm · warming

2 👥 Use suffixes to make adverbs, verbs and adjectives. The words in violet require changes in spelling:

people	**–er**	drive golf work manage paint read speak
	–or	conduct sail collect direct edit invent visit narrate
	–ist	art violin piano science
things	**–er**	time cook print record
nouns from adjectives	**–ness**	sad rude careless foolish gentle good kind
		nervous serious sweet sick friendly lonely
	–ity	similar sincere severe
	–ence	different confident innocent patient violent
nouns from verbs	**–ment**	disappoint develop agree pay replace enjoy move
	–ance	disappear accept appear resist insure
	–ion	act collect direct react protect investigate operate
	–ation	inform explain examine organize
	–ing	hear cook paint train type

3 👥 Fill the gaps with suitable words from above:

1 Cézanne was an .... who was a member of the Impressionist .... Many people get a lot of .... from looking at his ....s.

2 A surgeon is a doctor who carries out ....s. The work requires a lot of .... and many years of ....

3 The police have begun an .... into the .... of the star's wife, fearing that she may have been kidnapped. Because of the .... of the crime, their .... has been very swift. However, there may be an innocent .... for the whole affair.

4 The accident was due to the other ....'s .... Unfortunately, he was driving without .... and he refused to make .... for the repairs.

Weather and climate

Weather chaos

1 👥 Look at the title. What do you think the article is going to tell you?

2 Read the text and find the answers to these questions:

1 How many countries and states were affected by the most recent El Niño?
2 How many people died as a result of conditions brought on by El Niño?
3 What evidence does NOAA have that another El Niño is imminent?
4 Which region will be hit first?
5 How frequent are El Niño episodes?

New El Niño to bring weather chaos

A new El Niño, the periodic warming of the surface of the Pacific ocean that can trigger severe worldwide weather and environmental disasters, has been observed building up by the National Oceanic Atmospheric Administration in the USA.   1

The phenomenon brought droughts and floods, causing thousands of deaths and serious malnutrition, across Latin America, southern Africa and the Pacific region during its last appearance.   2

Some 230m people lost their homes in China, while a hurricane devastated Honduras. The phenomenon also caused serious delays to the monsoon in India and severe flooding in Bangladesh.   3

Scientists believe that the small rise in temperature in the Indian and Pacific oceans was enough to also provoke unusually severe cold weather in Europe in October and a devastating ice storm in the southern US.   4

Other phenomena included forest fires in Indonesia, Brazil, Central America and Florida, and floods in California and Mexico. More than fifteen per cent of the world's coral reefs were killed and the global tourism industry was hit.   5

Experts say it is too early to forecast the severity of this El Niño, but they expect the US to experience problems from this summer until next year. Scientists have predicted that El Niños will become more frequent and more severe as the world warms.   6

The NOAA warning is backed up by the increase in cloudiness and rainfall recorded recently over the equatorial central Pacific. The first region on the globe to experience El Niño's impacts would be in the tropical Pacific, according to the NOAA.   7

El Niño episodes have occurred every two to ten years and can last up to twelve months. In Spanish their name refers to Jesus Christ because they used to take place around Christmas.   8

John Vidal and Paul Brown

3 Highlight the words or phrases which mean the same as these:

¶1 occasional   start
¶2 very dry conditions   overflowing rivers
¶3 caused terrible damage
¶4 cause   terrible
¶7 serious effects
¶8 happened

🌐 Find out more
@ www.noaa.gov

4 👥 Discuss these questions:

• What for you is the worst kind of weather? Why?
• How do you find out about tomorrow's weather: from the radio? From TV? From the Internet? From a newspaper? Or do you ask someone?

Personal experiences

1 Ask each other the questions below to find out about times you remember which were . . .

particularly hot	unusually cold	extremely wet
very snowy	stormy and frightening	

- How did you feel? What did you do? How were you affected?
- How long did it last? What happened later?
- Have you been caught in a storm? Or caught in the snow? What happened?

2 Write sentences using these phrases, based on the experiences you talked about in 1.

```
Let me tell you about ...        Once I ...
What happened was ...            Have I told you about the time I ... ?
I remember the time ...          I'll never forget the time I ...
```

3 Write an e-mail or letter to a friend, telling him or her about a memorable experience where the weather played a part. (About 100 words.)

How do you mean?

1 Listen to Karen talking to David. Which of these phrases do they use?

> I don't quite understand.
> I don't really follow.
> I don't see what you mean.
> In what way?
> How do you mean?

> What I mean is . . .
> Let me say it another way . . .
> In other words . . .
> I mean . . .

2 Practise saying the phrases.

3 One of you should look at Activity 14 on page 134, the other at Activity 40 on page 142. You'll be talking about different aspects of the weather and climate.

'It must be summer,
the rain's warmer.'

Weather and climate

14A Living creatures

It's a wonderful world!

1 👥 **Look at the photos and discuss these questions:**

- What are your favourite animals?
- Do you enjoy visiting the zoo? Why/Why not?
- Do any members of your family have pets? What kind?
- What plants do you have inside and outside your home?

2 👥 **Add two more examples to each category:**

wild animals	rabbit	fox	....	....
farm animals	sheep	cow	....	....
birds	pigeon	duck	....	....
insects	bee	ant	....	....
fish	salmon	shark	....	....
reptiles	snake	crocodile	....	....
trees	palm	oak	....	....
fruit	orange	pineapple	....	....
flowers	rose	carnation	....	....

3 👥 **Do this questionnaire together:**

HOW GREEN ARE YOU?	You	Your partner
Do you ...		
recycle paper, glass and cans?		
use scrap paper instead of new paper for making notes?		
avoid buying over-packaged goods?		
avoid throwing things away if they can be re-used, repaired or recycled?		
pick up other people's litter?		
use public transport for long distances?		
use a bike or walk for short distances?		
turn off the lights when you leave a room?		
use low-energy light bulbs?		
make sure the heating isn't turned up too high in winter ?		
turn the air conditioning down in summer?		
avoid using too much water?		

4 👥 + 👥 Join another pair and compare your answers. Who is the 'greenest'?

Past simple and past continuous

1 First look at the examples in the Grammar reference section on page 127.

2 Write an answer to each question:

1 What were you doing when the alarm clock rang? *I was having a wonderful dream.*

And what did you do when it rang? *I woke up.*

2 What were you doing when the phone rang? ....

And what did you do when the phone rang? ....

3 What were you doing when the doorbell rang? ....

And what did you do when you heard it? ....

4 What were you doing when the lights went out? ....

And what did you do when they went out? ....

3 👥 Ask each other questions to find out what your partner was up to last week and at the times shown. Look at the examples below before you start, and follow the same pattern.

on	Tuesday	at 11 am	at 10 pm
	Wednesday	at 9 am	at 5 pm
	Thursday	at 2 pm	at midnight
	Friday	at 8 am	at 7 pm
	Saturday	at 7 am	at 11 pm
	Sunday	at noon	at 8 pm

What did you do on Monday last week?

— Oh, nothing special. I got up at the usual time, had breakfast and went to college. What about you?

Well, I didn't have any classes until after lunch. I stayed in bed till about 11 o'clock. And what were you doing at 4 pm on Thursday?

— At 4 pm? I was waiting for the bus home. What about you?

Me? Oh, I was . . .

Abbreviations and symbols, etc.

1 👥 Look at these abbreviations and symbols. Say them in full and explain their meanings:

titles:	Mr Mrs Dr Prof	*(or Mr. Mrs., etc.)*
addresses:	Ave Dr Gdns Rd Sq St	*(or Ave., Dr., etc.)*
measurements:	am pm hrs max min approx m kg	*(or a.m., p.m., etc.)*
technology:	CD TV DVD VCR PC WWW	*(but not C.D., T.V. etc.)*
countries, etc.:	USA UK GB EU UN NATO WWF	
symbols:	& $ £ % – / © ® Ø @ °C	

2 👥 Continue this sequence: Sun Mon ....

And this one: Jan Feb ....

3 👥 Note down five abbreviations that are commonly used in your own language. Explain their meanings in English.

The Eden Project

1 Read about the Eden Project before you listen to the interview:

Welcome to the Eden Project . . .

The Living Theatre of Plants & People

In a giant crater in Cornwall, in a reclaimed china clay quarry, you'll find the largest greenhouses in the world. Over 2 million visitors come to see them every year.

Inside: towering rainforests and tropical crops, the hot, dusty Mediterranean with citrus groves and gnarled cork oaks.

Outside: crops and landscapes of Chile, Cornwall and the Indian Hills.

Why? To set the stage where science, art and technology blend to tell the story of our place in nature and, working with partners, look to our possible positive futures.

The Eden Project: testimony to the fact that if you dare to dream you can make a difference.

2 Listen to the interview with Sue Hill, artistic director of the Eden Project. Decide which statements are true or false, according to her:

1 The Eden Project uses artists to tell the stories of the plants.
2 One of the greenhouses houses a tropical rainforest.
3 Tea is grown inside the Mediterranean greenhouse.
4 Visitors can see sugar and cocoa actually growing.
5 Tim Smit, the founder of the Eden Project, used to be a film producer.
6 He wanted to show people the intimate relationship they have with plants.
7 The Millennium Commission supported the project to celebrate the new millennium in 2000.
8 Most visitors leave the Eden Project feeling guilty and pessimistic.

3 Discuss these questions:

- Would you like to visit the Eden Project? Why/Why not?
- What more would you like to know about it?

Find out more @
www.edenproject.org.uk

Comparing

Have you ever written on a banana in biro? It's crazy but it works like a dream. You wish all writing could be this way. It flows. It's smooth. It's sensual. You get the urge to write poems; sonnets; odes to lilies. A strongly worded letter of complaint is impossible. It makes you realise that everything can be improved. That even the familiar can be looked at in a new light. And that imagination is more powerful than knowledge. Do you believe in the power of dreams? HONDA

1 👥 **Read the banana above, then discuss these questions:**

- What seems to be the very best thing about writing on a banana?
- This is an advertisement for Honda cars – what does it say about the cars?
- What are the disadvantages of writing on a banana?

2 👥 **Discuss the differences between:**

- writing on normal paper *and* writing on a banana
- using a pencil *and* using a ballpoint (biro) *and* using a fountain pen
- word-processing on a computer *and* writing in an exercise book
- writing without making notes first *and* making notes before writing.

3 ✎ **Write about the pleasures of writing on a computer in the same style as the text above.**

Follow-up questions

1 🔊 👥 **Listen to Brian talking to Kevin. What questions could encourage Kevin to say more?**

🔊 **Now listen to Julie talking to Kevin. Does she ask any questions you thought of?**

2 🔊 **Practise saying the phrases on the right.**

Did you have a good trip?	Yes.	Tell me about it.
		What was good about it?
Did the trip take a long time?	Yes.	How long exactly did it take?
		Why did it take so long?
Were you alone?	No.	Who went with you?
		How many people were with you?
Did you arrive on time?	No.	When exactly did you arrive?
		Why were you late?

3 👥 **One of you should look at Activity 9 on page 133, the other at Activity 28 on page 138. You'll be encouraging each other to say more.**

Nature

15A Hobbies and games

So much to do, so little time!

1 👥 **Discuss these questions:**

- Do you collect anything: stamps, CDs, books, shoes, hats, etc.?
  What do you collect – and why?
- Do you have any creative hobbies: photography, making things, etc.?
- If you had more time, what new hobby would you most like to take up?

2 👥 **Imagine you have a whole evening alone to do what you like. Number these activities 1 to 12 to show which you'd prefer to do:**

....	clean your room	....	read a magazine or newspaper
....	cook a nice meal	....	sit alone and think
....	listen to music	....	surf the Internet
....	play a computer game	....	watch a video or DVD
....	play a musical instrument	....	watch television
....	read a book	....	write letters or e-mails to friends

- Which of your favourite activities are missing from the list above?
- If you were with a friend, not alone, what would you do on such an evening?

3 👥 **Are you a sporty person? Do this questionnaire together:**

In an average month, how often do you play or take part in these sports? Give yourself a score (0 to 5) for each sport:

never–0 · hardly ever–1 · sometimes–2 · quite a lot–3 · whenever I can–4 · all the time–5

(If your favourite sport is missing, add it to the end of the list.)

aerobics	☐	gymnastics	☐	swimming	☐
basketball	☐	running	☐	tennis	☐
cycling	☐	sailing	☐	volleyball	☐
dancing	☐	skating	☐	walking	☐
football	☐	skiing	☐	windsurfing	☐
Frisbee	☐	snowboarding	☐	working out	☐
golf	☐	surfing	☐		☐

Add up your scores, then look at Activity 27 on page 138 for an evaluation of your total.

Past perfect

1 First look at the examples in the Grammar reference section on page 127.

2 👥 Complete the reported sentences:

1 'I've never met Bill.' She told me that *she had never met Bill* .

2 'I've always wanted to meet him.' She told me that ....

3 'We arranged to meet on Friday.' She told me that ....

4 'I arrived early.' She told me that ....

5 'I waited for over an hour.' She told me that ....

6 'He never showed up.' She told me that ....

3 👥 Fill the gaps in these stories, using appropriate forms of the verbs in blue:

1 It was my first visit to a football match. I *had* .... never .... one
before. Well, I .... my brother play at school, but that doesn't
count. We .... our tickets in advance, to make sure we .... good
seats. Before half time our team .... already .... a goal. But
by the end of the match the other side .... and just before
the final whistle ...., they .... another goal.
We all .... very disappointed.

attend
watch
buy   get
score
equalize
blow   get
feel

2 They .... already .... their meal by the time I .... They
.... all the food and ....n't even .... me any bread.
I .... pretty cross because this .... the previous time
I .... home late and I ....n't .... that it would happen again!

finish   arrive
eat   leave
feel   happen
get   expect

'False friends'

1 👥 Explain the difference in meaning between these words:

👁️ 'False friends' are words which are similar in English and in your language, but which actually have different meanings.

actually	and	now 'Actually' means 'in fact'. 'Now' means 'at this moment'.
agenda		notebook
assist		attend
conference		lecture
control		check
cry		shout
eventual		possible
experience		experiment
a game		a play
lecture		reading
library		bookshop
parent		relative
pass an exam		take an exam
professor		teacher
sensible		sensitive
smoking		dinner jacket/tuxedo
sympathetic		likeable, friendly, nice

2 👥 How many of the above are 'false friends'
in your language?

Think of some more English 'false friends'
in your language.

Free time

Arthur Melin

1 Complete this chart with information from the article:

	first popular	number sold	invented by
Frisbee			
Superball			
Hula-Hoop			
Instant Fish			

Arthur Melin – *The man who brought us the Hula-Hoop and the Frisbee*

Few people in the history of fun has been as successful as Arthur 'Spud' Melin, who has died aged 77, the co-inventor of the Hula-Hoop and manufacturer of the Frisbee, the Superball and lots more crazy games.

He and his boyhood pal, later business partner, Richard 'Rich' Knerr, were students at the University of South California. The founded the Wham-O company operating first in Knerr's Los Angeles garage. They made and sold toy guns, boomerangs and other toys by mail order. Their Air Blaster could blow out a candle 8 metres away.

The Frisbee was their first major success, but it wasn't their invention. Students at Yale University started the craze by throwing empty metal pie tins from the Frisbie Baking Company. In 1948 Fred Morrison, a building inspector, developed a plastic version and in 1951 started manufacturing what he called the 'Flyin' Saucer'. It did not sell well, but Morrison demonstrated it to Wham-O in 1955. Melin and Knerr bought the novelty for $1m (plus lifetime royalties for Morrison). At first they called it the 'Fling Saucer'. In 1958, they renamed it the 'Frisbee'.

In the 1960s the Frisbee was popular with hippies and with guys trying to impress their girls with frisbee flips – 'Flat flip flies straight. Tilted flip curves. When a ball dreams, it dreams it's a Frisbee,' they said. A hundred million Frisbees have been sold, and as Melin hoped, they became a sport – the basis of the team game Ultimate, with its own world championships.

Wham-O's most famous contribution to silliness, the Hula-Hoop, was born in 1957. A visiting Australian mentioned to Melin how, back home as a kid, he had rotated a bamboo hoop around his waist in gym class. Melin developed this idea, and, after prototype tests with Pasadena children, Wham-O started making millions of lightweight hollow plastic cylinders. Melin and Knerr explained that the mechanical principle behind it depended on the ratio of waist to diameter: 'Small hoops or big waists just won't work'. In the summer of 1958, the craze sold 40 million $1.98 hoops.

Wham-O kept an open door to inventors: 20 nutty ideas arrived daily. In the early 1960s Norman Stingley, a chemical engineer, showed them some plastic, Zectron, which bounced uncontrollably. After two years of development this was marketed as the springy Superball. A giant Superball accidentally dropped from a 23rd-floor hotel room window, bounced back 15 floors and destroyed a parked car as it fell again. The ball was undamaged. Twenty million Superballs were sold.

One of Melin's ideas which didn't succeed was his Instant Fish. On a trip to Africa he discovered a species of fish which laid eggs in mud during the dry season. When the rains came, the eggs hatched and little fish swam away. You just needed to add water to mud to get an instant aquarium. Unfortunately, the fish he brought back to America wouldn't produce any eggs – so that was the end of a great idea.

1
2
3
4
5
6
7

Find out more @
www.wham-o.com

2 Highlight the words or phrases which mean the same as these:

¶2   friend
¶3   fashion, fad   payments
¶5   experimental product
¶6   crazy   went up and down

3 👥 Discuss these questions:

- Can you remember any crazes from when you were younger?
- What sports or games are most popular or fashionable now?

Writing a story Writing

1 ✏️ 👥 How can you improve these stories to make them more exciting?

> Our car broke down on a quiet road. We waited a long time until someone came who could give us a lift. It was getting dark. We were happy when someone came.

> Bob met Annie on a blind date. At first they didn't like each other. They went on another date and had a row. In the end they fell in love.

> I hadn't played football before but the team was a player short. At the end of the match I was standing near the goal. Another player kicked the ball and it hit me on the head. The ball went into the goal. We won the match.

👥 + 👥 Join another pair and compare your improvements.

2 ✏️ Write the story of a film, book or personal experience. Try to make the story sound exciting!

Emphasis Speaking

1 🔊 Listen to the conversations and <u>underline</u> the words that are emphasized in the answers:

Was the match exciting?	— Exciting? Yes, it was very exciting! I've never seen such an exciting match.
Was it a romantic movie?	— Wow, yes. It was really romantic! I've never seen such a romantic movie!
Was there enough food?	— Oh, yes! There was loads of food! There was so much food that we all ate far too much!

2 🔊 Practise saying the answers in the same way.

3 👥 Ask each other these questions, and use the phrases on the right in your answers.

Did you have fun?	lots of
Has he got a lot of money?	loads of plenty of lots and lots of
Have we got enough time?	
Was it a good book?	very
Did you have a bad journey?	
Was it a difficult exam?	
Are you happy?	really ever so extremely

Free time

71

11–15 Revision

Topic vocabulary

11 There are 20 inventions and tools in this puzzle. Can you find them all?

```
h i c n r e n s e o e o n o c c g s e c n a n c
g e n h e c v i d e o r e c o r d e r e t l b g
a e c m m t n d v d p l a y e r o c c y n a a s
d n o o o n o d i s h w a s h e r y y e y r l n
g e o b t w a l k m a n c l e c t c c h m l t
e n h i e o o c o r k s c r e w t e y i c p e
t e s l c i p e n c i l s h a r p e n e r l o l
t e c e o c c l y c y y y h y n l e l y s o i e
e g i p n k l e t o o l y a g p e g m c e c n v
c o s h t e y s o c h h n m t c l s n a o k t i
h c s o r t o l s h c e g m l o e i c n i n p s
l c o n o t l s h e n s h e e e y h e o c l e l
o e r e l l o s c r e w d r i v e r e r n e n o
h e s h s e o i p a p e r c l i p c s o s o g n
```

13–14 Try this crossword puzzle:

Across
- **2** Light rain
- **4** Heavy rain
- **7** A baby cat
- **8** Strong wind
- **11** Bees and ants are ....
- **12** Wet snow
- **13** Overflowing rivers
- **14** You can see animals here
- **15** Jungle
- **16** Warm building with transparent roof

Down
- **1** A baby dog
- **3** Children call them 'bunnies'
- **4** No rain for a long time
- **5** Light wind
- **6** Snakes and crocodiles are ....
- **9** Hot weather
- **10** Thunder and ....
- **12** Rainfall, but soon over

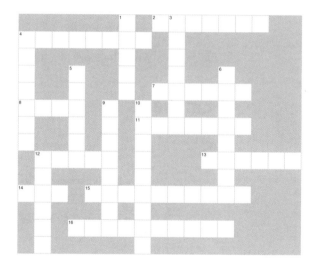

Grammar review

A Fill each gap with a suitable word or phrase (use the verbs in grey, where necessary):

11 MP3 ....<u>invent</u>.......... by Karlheinz Brandenburg, head of the multimedia department of the Fraunhofer Institute in Germany. The MP3 algorithm ....<u>use</u>.............. to process audio files digitally. Large audio files ....<u>compress</u>.......... into a much smaller size. This makes it possible for near-CD quality music to ....<u>download</u>.......... from the Web.

12 If I .... a rich uncle, he .... give me some money. If he .... me £1,000, I .... spend any of it, I .... save it so that I .... go on holiday to somewhere exotic. I .... probably go to Greece, and I .... all summer there, relaxing. But I know this .... happen, so I .... probably stay at home. If the weather .... nice, I .... go to the beach.

The numbers (11–15) show the unit where the grammar points were first introduced.

13 My friend asked me what the weather .... like the next day. She wanted to know .... rain. I asked her why .... know, but she .... tell me.

14 When I .... out of the window I .... that it .... already quite late. Out in the street two boys .... with a Frisbee and nearby two women .... an argument until one of them .... away looking angry. A motorist .... to park a long car in a very short space, and I .... on watching until he eventually .... up and .... away . . .

15 After the first motorist ....*drive*.......... away, a shorter car ....*stop*.......... in the road. The driver ....*reverse*.......... into the parking space, then he ....*get*.......... out of the car and ....*go*.......... into a shop. While he ....*be*.......... in the shop a young man ....*open*.......... the door of the car, ...*start*.......... the engine, and ....*drive*.......... it away – the man .... not only ....*forget*.......... to lock the car but he ....*leave*.......... his keys in the ignition!

Rewrite the sentences, using the words in red:

B

11 No-one has ever cleaned this room.   never
This room ....

12 I can't clean it because I don't have enough time.   more
If I .... clean it.

13 'Will someone clean it if I give them some money?' she asked.   paid
She wondered .... them.

14 At lunchtime I hadn't finished cleaning the room.   still
I .... the room at lunchtime.

15 I cleaned the room but then she forgot to pay me.   after
She didn't .... the room.

Vocabulary development and pronunciation

Write your answers to these questions:

11 **Form adjectives from these words:**

enjoy *enjoyable* hunger sun prefer help accident

12 **What nationality is a person from these countries?**

Poland *Polish* Greece Egypt France Spain Ireland Switzerland

13 **Form nouns from these words:**

act *action* different explain insure careless innocent enjoy

14 **Write these abbreviations in full:**

St *Street* max Sq Feb Wed UK approx 100m

15 **Fill in the missing words with 'false friends':**

a) My mother is one of my .... , my aunt is one of my ....

b) How many students .... the ....'s .... at the university?

c) She is very .... , and she may cry if you .... at her.

d) They .... my passport at the airport.

Good health

1 👥 **Look at the pictures and discuss these questions:**

- What would you say to the people in the photos?
- What do you do to keep fit and stay healthy?

2 👥 **Fill the gaps in these sentences with a suitable word or phrase:**

1 If your tooth hurts, make an a .... to see the d ....

2 If you have a cold you'll probably just c .... and s................ a lot.
   If you really have flu you have a splitting h............................. and feel s..................

3 Before going to Africa, she had to have i.....................................s against various tropical
   d................s. And she had to take anti-malaria t................s.

4 The doctor asked her p................. how he felt.

5 If someone has been i........................ in an accident you should call an a..............................!

6 I get a p................. in my back if I study for too long.

3 👥 **Write the names of six more parts in each 'zone' of this person's body:**

........chin....lips..

....

........little..finger....elbow...

....

........heel....big..toe..

....

4 👥 **What would you do if . . .**

. . . you felt sick?   . . . you had a headache?
. . . someone fainted?   . . . you broke your arm?
. . . you couldn't sleep?   . . . your back hurt?
. . . you had a cold?   . . . you twisted your ankle?
. . . you thought you had flu?   . . . you were completely unfit?

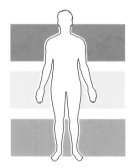
Find out more @
www.health.com +
www.healthfinder.gov +
www.nhsdirect.nhs.uk

Articles and quantifiers – 2

1 First look at the examples in the Grammar reference section on pages 120 and 121.

2 👥 What is the difference in meaning between the phrases in red?

The police in the UK don't have guns.   I asked a police officer for directions.
Is Alaska a country or a state?   They live in the country.
I'd like an apple.   I'd like some apples.   I like apples.
We went to the island by sea and stayed in a nice hotel by the sea.
You can't catch a cold from the cold.

3 👥 Spot the mistakes in these sentences and correct them:

1 I have problem, can you give me an advice, please?
2 The new cars cost more than second-hand ones.
3 If you have high temperature, you'd better go to the bed.
4 To become doctor you have to study the medicine.
5 Do you go to school by the bus or on the foot?
6 If you have headache take a aspirin.

4 👥 Add a, an or *the* in the gaps – but ONLY where necessary!

1 Normally I love .... music, but I really don't like .... music she plays.
2 I usually drink .... water with .... meals, but I prefer .... water you get in .... bottles to .... water you get from .... tap.
3 He wanted to be .... dentist but he didn't have .... right qualifications to get onto .... course.
4 .... best way to stay in .... good health is to take plenty of .... exercise and eat .... healthy food. And don't smoke .... cigarettes. .... yoga is more relaxing than .... aerobics and helps to reduce .... stress.
5 .... United States is on .... other side of .... Atlantic from .... Europe. .... state of .... California is in .... West on .... Pacific Coast.

Stréssing the corréct sýllable

1 Mark the stressed syllable in these words:

áccident   accidéntally   actually   excellent   marvellous   modern   normally   occasionally
particularly   probably   unfortunately

🔊 Now listen to the recording and check your answers.

2 👥 Mark the stressed syllable in these words. Check your answers in **Activity 20** on page 136.

appóintment   dóctor   exam   examination   gymnastics   hospital   information   medicine
operation   politics   professor   pronunciation   qualifications   temperature   treatment

3 👥 Mark the stressed syllable in these months. Then check your answers in **Activity 44** on page 143.

Jánuary   February   April   July   August   September   October   November

Now, to practise, say all 12 months in reverse order, starting with 'December'.

4 👥 Look back through the last few pages of this book. Find FIVE multi-syllable words, write them down, mark the stressed syllable and say them aloud.

Examples: photógraphy   sympathetic

Keeping fit

At the gym

1 Match the words and phrases in blue with the definitions in red:

rewards   difficulties
hurdles   disadvantage
firm   make my heart beat faster
like-minded people   people who have the same attitude
worn out   satisfying advantages
down side   strict
get my heart rate up   tablets to give you extra vitamins
vitamin supplements   tired

2 Listen to the interviews with Andy, a fitness instructor, and one of his clients, Rachel. Correct the mistakes in these sentences:

1 Andy finds that his professional attitude makes it harder for clients.
2 Andy always speaks softly to his clients.
3 Andy doesn't meet many healthy people during his work.
4 It takes two weeks for people to feel the effects of their training.
5 Andy says there is one disadvantage to keeping fit.
6 Rachel found yoga a very effective way of keeping fit.
7 She goes to the gym once a week and spends three hours there.
8 Although she has a fitness instructor she often feels bored at the gym.
9 Rachel always feels like a session at the gym.
10 Andy never shouts at Rachel.

3 Discuss these questions:
- What would you enjoy and not enjoy about Andy's job?
- What are some other ways of keeping fit, apart from going to a gym?
- Who do you know who keeps really fit? What does he or she do?

Giving advice

1 What advice would you give someone on how to lead a longer, healthier life? Number these ideas in order of importance (1 = most important, 10 = least important). Add two more ideas at the end of the list:

☐	drink two litres of water a day	☐	don't worry too much
☐	don't smoke	☐	do something enjoyable every day
☐	eat plenty of fruit and vegetables	☐	sleep eight hours a night
☐	go to the gym every day	☐	walk as often as possible
☐	take vitamin tablets	☐	
☐	don't eat junk food	☐	

2 Practise saying these phrases:

> *You could swim twice a week.*
> *Have you thought of taking up swimming?*
> *Swimming is a good idea.*
> *I think you should take up swimming.*
> *Why not take up swimming?*
> *One thing you could do is take up swimming.*

Use the same phrases to recommend the activities in the chart above.

3 Look at the pictures and fill the gaps in the instructions using the words in the list.

Then try the exercises yourselves, helping each other to get them right.

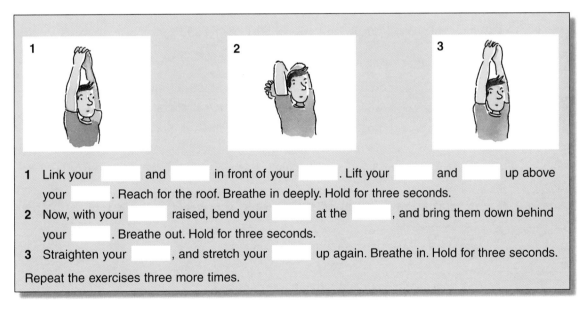

1 Link your ____ and ____ in front of your ____ . Lift your ____ and ____ up above your ____ . Reach for the roof. Breathe in deeply. Hold for three seconds.

2 Now, with your ____ raised, bend your ____ at the ____ , and bring them down behind your ____ . Breathe out. Hold for three seconds.

3 Straighten your ____ , and stretch your ____ up again. Breathe in. Hold for three seconds.

Repeat the exercises three more times.

arms
chest
elbows
fingers
hands
head

4 One of you should look at Activity 10 on page 133, the other at Activity 30 on page 139. You'll be asking for and giving more advice.

5 How would you feel if you received this e-mail from a friend?

▶ Attachments: none

[Courier ▼] [Larger ▼] **B** *I* U T ▤ ▤ ▤ ▤ ▤ ▤ ▤ ▦**A** ▾ ◈ ▾ —

You're stupid not to take any exercise. You'll get very fat and
everybody will laugh at you. And it's ridiculous to eat so much
junk food — everyone knows it's bad for your health. If you had
any brains you'd eat more healthy food, particularly fruit and
vegetables. Pull yourself together and don't be such an idiot.

✎ Rewrite the e-mail in a much less hostile style! Add some more recommendations.

Good health

77

Puzzling it out

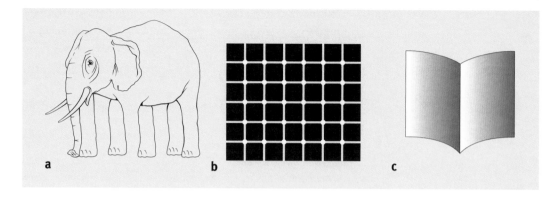

a   b   c

1 👥 **Look at the pictures and discuss these questions:**

- How many legs does the elephant have?
- How many black dots are there? And how many white dots? (Count them aloud in English.)
- Is the book face up or face down?

2 👥 **Which of the sentences below is hardest to read, and why?**

a   .srehto naht evlos ot redrah hcum era selzzup emoS

b   An optical illusion confuses the brain so that you can't trust your eyes.

c   I find it very hard to solve a puzzle that has numbers in it.

3 👥 **Work together to solve these puzzles:**

a   What are the next two numbers in this sequence: **31 28 31 30** .... ?

b   What are the next two letters in this sequence: **O T T F F S S** .... ?

c   What are the next two letters in this sequence: **Y Y H L Y E Y** .... ?

d   What occurs once in a minute, twice in a week and once in a year?

e   If a clock strikes the hour every hour, how many times does it strike in one day?

f   Can you read this coded message?

   19 15 13 5   16 21 26 26 12 5 19   1 18 5   8 1 18 4 5 18   20 8 1 14   15 20 8 5 18 19

g   Can you read this coded message?

   W2LLD4N2 Y45H1V2F3N3SH2DTH2S2P5ZZL2S

4 👥 + 👥 **Join another pair and compare your answers.**

If there's time, write your own coded message for another group to decode.

MARTIN GUHL

If . . . sentences – 2

1 First look at the examples in the Grammar reference section on page 126.

2 👥 What is the difference in meaning between these sentences?

1 If I knew the answer I would tell you.   If I had known the answer I would have told you.
2 What would you do if the lights went out?   What will you do if the lights go out?
3 If we run out of money what can we do?   If we ran out of money what could we do?

3 👥 Spot the mistakes in these sentences and correct them:

1 I would have phoned her if I would have known her number.
2 What would you have done if you missed the last bus home yesterday?
3 If I was born in England, I'd have learnt English as a child.
4 I wouldn't solve the problem unless I didn't have some help.

4 👥 Complete the sentences, following the same pattern as the example:

1 I didn't know all the answers, so I didn't get 100%.
   But if I had known all the answers, I would have got 100%.

2 I didn't have enough money, so I couldn't buy the CD.
   But if ....

3 My computer crashed, so I lost all my work.
   But if ....

4 We didn't have a map, so we lost our way.
   But if ....

5 We didn't stay at home, so we got soaking wet in the rain.
   But if ....

6 He ate so much ice cream that he felt very sick.
   But if ....

Make, take and *do*

1 👥 Add *made, took* or *did* in the gaps:

1 We .... the exercise very quickly, but we .... several mistakes.
2 My sister .... her school-leaving exams last year.
3 He .... a ten-minute break and .... the crossword puzzle.
4 She .... a phone call to her boyfriend while I .... some work.
5 We .... the washing-up while my friend .... us some coffee.
6 They .... such a mess that it .... us all laugh!

2 👥 Two phrases in each box are wrong and should be in a different box. Move them to the correct box:

make		**do**		**take**	
a cake		a crossword puzzle		a break	
a film		a lot of work		a bus	
a mess		a noise		a look	
a mistake		a photo		a promise	
a phone call		an exercise		a shower	
a rest		some cleaning		a tablet	
some bread		some damage		a train	
some coffee		some shopping		an appointment	
someone laugh		some work		your time	
the washing-up		something well			
		your best			

3 ✏️ 👥 Write FIVE sentences, each using two phrases from the boxes.

Stretch your brain

1 👥 Work together to solve these problems. Deal with the easier ones first, then come back to the ones you find harder. You'll need to read each one carefully!

A   Six glasses are in a row. The first three are full of juice; the second three are empty. By moving only one glass, can you arrange them so that empty and full glasses alternate?

B   You and a group of your friends are in the library. One friend says there is a £100 note hidden between pages 75 and 76 of a book in the library. But you decide not to go and look for it. Why?

C   Which word in the English language is most frequently spelt wrong?

D   This is an unusual paragraph. I'm curious how quickly you can find out what is so unusual about it. It looks so plain you would think nothing was wrong with it! In fact, nothing is wrong with it! It is unusual though. Study it, and think about it, but you still may not find anything odd. But if you work at it a bit, you might find out! Try to do this without any aid!

E   You need to measure one litre of water, but you only have a five-litre bottle and a three-litre jug. What do you do?

F   How would you rearrange the letters in the phrase 'new door' to make one word? (There is only one correct answer.)

G   At noon and midnight the hour and minute hands on a clock are exactly coincident with each other. How many other times between noon and midnight do the hour and minute hands cross?

H   If you were to spell out numbers, how far would you have to go until you found the letter 'A'?

I   All my sweaters are red, except two. All my sweaters are blue, except two. All my sweaters are green, except two. How many sweaters do I have?

2 👥 + 👥 Compare your answers. Then discuss these questions:

- Which puzzle was hardest for you? Why?
- Which were easy and why?
- Did the puzzles get easier, the more you did?

🌐 Find more brainteasers, riddles and puzzles @ www.braingle.com

Spoting mistakes – 1

1 👥 Find the mistakes in these paragraphs and correct them. Each paragraph illustrates a different kind of mistake.

Try to solve the puzzles together!

👁 In writing people are more likely to notice your mistakes than when you speak. Before sending a message, or submitting homework, it's important to check your work and correct any mistakes.

> You find shellter in a mountin hutt on a windey night. You need to light a fire to get worm. There is plenty of would, but only won match, one peace of newspaper and one candle. What do you light first?

> A woman was sleep in a hotel. In middle of night she wake up and can't go back to sleep. She pick up the phone and making a phone call. She hang up and go to sleep again. Who she called and why?

> A town has only two hair salons? One has a broken mirror dirty floor covered in hair torn magazines and the hairdresser has a terrible haircut. The other has a new mirror clean floor new magazines and a hairdresser with a great haircut. Where would you go and why!

> Last week I was able to turn the bedroom light off and get into bed before the room was darkness. The bed and the light button are two metres separate. Can you estimate how I did this?

👁 A computer spell-checker won't spot these mistakes:

A dog wags it's tale when its happy.

The whether will bee sunny at the end off the weak.

The first person who guest the answer one the price.

Your going too need a bigger boat

What kind of mistakes were illustrated in each paragraph?

(The solutions to the puzzles are in Activity 17 on page 135).

2 👥 Look at your two most recent pieces of homework and discuss these questions:

- What kind of mistakes did you both make most: spelling, grammar, punctuation, or vocabulary?
- How many of those mistakes could you have corrected if you had checked your work more carefully before submitting it?

Repetition and clarification

1 🔊 👥 Listen to the conversation and put a tick by the phrases that are used.

> *Could you say that again, please?*
> *I'm sorry, I didn't catch what you said.*
> *Sorry, I don't quite understand.*
> *I don't quite follow.*
> *Sorry, did you say . . . or . . . ?*
> *Does that mean the same as . . . ?*
> *I'm not with you.*

> *Let me put it another way . . .*
> *I'll just explain that again.*

2 🔊 👥 Practise saying the phrases.

3 👥 Explain to your partner how to get from where you are now to various well-known buildings in your town or city. Use the phrases above to encourage each other to repeat and clarify any puzzling or confusing information.

The 21st century

 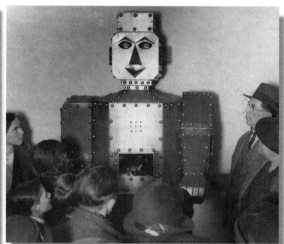

1 👥 **Look at the pictures and discuss these questions:**

🌐 Find out more @ www.bbc.co.uk/ science/robots + inventors.about.com

- How did machines change people's lives in the 20th century? (Think of vehicles, labour-saving devices, entertainment, computers, etc.)
- How will they change our lives in the 21st century?
- If you could have a robot assistant, what would you like it to do for you?

2 👥 **Fill the gaps in these sentences with words from below:**

1 If you want to know the .... of rain, listen to the weather ....
2 Nobody can .... what the future will ....
3 I .... to get a good job when I finish my studies and begin my ....
4 I didn't .... that this would happen. Nobody ....
5 Her .... is to become president one day. She is being rather ....!
6 I'm .... going to the country this weekend.

ambition	bring	career	expect	forecast	hope	likelihood
looking forward to		optimistic	predict	saw it coming		

3 👥 **We can never be certain what the future may bring.**
Number the statements in order of probability (1 = most likely to go, 6 = least likely to go).

.... *Al's definitely going to Austria.*
.... *Bob may not go to Belgium.*
.... *Carl might just possibly go to Cambridge.*
.... *Nina may go to New Zealand.*
.... *Olive's very unlikely to go to Oxford.*
.... *Pam probably won't go to Panama.*

4 👥 + 👥 **First, work in separate pairs. Make a list of cities, countries or islands, each beginning with a different letter of the alphabet.**

One pair's list should go from **A** (e.g. Antarctica) to **M** (e.g. Madrid).
The other pair's list should go from **N** (e.g. Norway) to **Z** (e.g. Zambia).

Join the other pair and decide how likely it is that you'll visit the places, using the phrases in **3**.

For and *since*

1 First look at the examples in the Grammar reference section on page 127.

2 👥 **What is the difference in meaning between these pairs of sentences?**

She has lived there for four years.
I have been reading this book.
Someone has been drinking my milk.

She lived there for four years.
I have read this book.
Someone has drunk my milk.

3 👥 **Spot the mistakes in these sentences and correct them:**

1 How many biscuits have you been eating?   *How many biscuits have you eaten?*
2 She has been studied in London since two years.
3 I am not drinking milk since two years ago.
4 I have only been reading ten pages of the book until now.

4 👥 **Fill the gaps in these sentences, using the verbs in grey and *for* or *since* if necessary.**

1 How long .... you ....^study........... English?
2 How many pages of the book .... you .....^read......... so far?
3 It's such a good film that I ....^see......... it three times.
4 He ....^visit......... five different countries so far this year.
5 You're very late, we ....^wait................. here .... almost an hour.
6 They ....^play......... basketball .... lunchtime – and they're still playing!
7 The phone ....^ring........... for ages but nobody ....^answer................. it.
8 We ....^discuss........... the future .... the beginning of this lesson.

British and American English

1 👥 **Match these British words to their American equivalents:**

👁 Apart from some minor spelling differences, the main differences between British English and American English are vocabulary. Thanks to Hollywood, British people understand most American words. But many Americans don't understand British words.

🇬🇧	🇺🇸
biscuit	bathroom, restroom
boot (of a car)	candy
city centre	cookie
colleague	co-worker
CV	downtown
first floor	elevator
ground floor	first floor
fortnight	second floor
holiday	gas
public holiday	freeway, highway
lift (in a building)	pants
motorway	résumé
petrol	schedule
sweets	trunk
timetable	two weeks
toilet	vacation
trousers	holiday

In Britain they say 'biscuit'. What do they say in America?
— I think they say 'cookie'.

What do they call the boot of a car in America?
— I think they call it the trunk.

🌐 Find out more @ www.travelfurther.net/ dictionaries

2 👥 **Here are some more American terms. 'Translate' them into British English:**

02/29/04	area code	ZIP code
Daylight Saving Time	Monday through Friday	ten after six
sidewalk	subway	windshield
color	center	neighbor

The future

Hopes and ambitions

Five years from now . . .

1 🔊 We asked Tony, Amy, Daniel and Sarah to tell us what they hope or expect to be doing five years from now. Listen to their predictions and complete the chart below.

Tony, 25, is a graphic designer

Amy, 16, is at school

Sarah, 19, is on her 'gap year' before uni

Daniel, 20, is studying sports at uni

	five years from now		
	work or uni	free time	relationships
Tony			
Amy			
Daniel			
Sarah			

2 👥 Compare you answers. Then interview each other and discuss these questions:

- What will you be doing five years from now?
- What work will you be doing ten years from now?
- What are your ambitions? What are your career plans?
- What are the advantages and disadvantages of making plans for your future?

'You will get old and wrinkled and moan about the weather.'

For and against

1 👥 Read this very short composition. What extra advantages would you add? And what extra disadvantages would you add?

> PLANNING YOUR FUTURE
> Making plans for the future is a good idea because you have to
> have some idea of where your life is going. If you don't make any
> plans you just drift along and are unlikely to be successful.
>   However, as it's impossible to predict what the future will
> bring, an inflexible scheme is not a good idea. You have to have
> alternatives up your sleeve in case things don't go according to
> plan.

2 👥 Discuss the pros and cons of these future predictions. Would they improve life in the future, or make it worse?

There will be no armies

Hydrogen will replace petrol as a fuel

Public transport will be free

Everyone will live to be 100 years old

There will be no exams

More leisure time: weekends will last four days

3 ✏️ Write a composition on one of the topics you discussed in 2. Here are some phrases you can use:

```
One advantage of ... is ...          However, ...
... is a good idea because ...       On the other hand, ...
I am in favour of ... because ...    The main disadvantage of ... is ...
... would be great because ...       I am against ... because ...
                                     The main drawback of ... is ...
                                     ... is not such a good idea because...
```

Telephoning

1 👥 Discuss these questions:

- How many phone calls do you make per day on average?
- How many text messages do you send and receive?
- What do you like and dislike about using the phone?
- How would you feel if you had to make a phone call in English?

2 🔊 👥 Practise saying these phrases:

> *Could I speak to ..., please?*
> *Could you ask her to phone me, please?*
> *My name is ... and my number is ...*
> *Can I call you back in a few minutes?*
> *Thank you for calling.*
> *Nice to talk to you.' Bye.*

> *She's not here. Can I take a message?*
> *Who's calling, please?*
> *It's a very bad line. Can you say that again?*
> *This is ... speaking.*
> *You're breaking up. I'll call you back.*

3 👥 One of you should look at Activity 11 on page 134, the other at Activity 31 on page 139. You'll be making some phone calls. Don't sit facing each other – don't make eye contact or use gestures.

The future

85

Earning a living

A suitable job?

Speaking and vocabulary

1 👥 **Look at the photos and discuss these questions:**

- Would you like either of the jobs shown? Why (not)?
- What are some jobs that are mostly done by men? Why?
- What are some jobs that are mostly done by women? Why?
- Are there any jobs that should *never* be done by men? Or *never* by women?

2 👥 **Look at the jobs in red. Discuss who works in the different workplaces:**

actor	in a bank
architect	factory
assembly line worker	hospital
builder	hotel
caretaker	recording studio
cashier	restaurant
chambermaid	school
chef	shop
cleaner	television studio
farmer	theatre
flight attendant	university
lecturer	
lifeguard	in an office
machine operator	
manager	outdoors
musician	
nurse	on a beach
postman	building site
producer	farm
receptionist	plane
seaman	ship
shop assistant	
surgeon	
waiter/waitress	

> *An actor works in a theatre.*
> *— Or in a television studio.*
> *OK, where does an architect work?*
> *— In an office.*
> *Yes. Or on a building site.*

3 👥 + 👥 **Compare your answers. Then discuss these questions:**

- Can you think of more jobs that are done in the workplaces listed?
- Which of the jobs would you not like to do? Why?

Relative clauses

1 First look at the examples in the Grammar reference section on page 128.

2 👥 Decide what is the difference in meaning between these sentences:

The man who told me about you.
She is the person that you need to see.
My friend, whose name is Tim, lives nearby.

The man you told me about.
She is the person who needs to see you.
My friend whose name is Tim lives nearby.

3 👥 Spot the mistakes in these sentences and correct them:

1 Her father who has lived alone since her mother died will be 80 this year.
2 I didn't get the job what I wanted.
3 The woman which you spoke to is the manager.
4 The man, who is wearing glasses, is her assistant.
5 My best friend who's name is Tim is moving to America which is a long way from here.

4

👥 One of you should look at **Activity 12** on page 134, the other at **Activity 32** on page 140. You'll have more information about the people in the pictures to share, following this pattern:

> *What's the name of the man who is wearing a bow tie?*
> *— That's Mr Jones.*
> *Oh, Mr Jones, right. I think he's the man who interviewed me for a job.*

Words with similar meanings

1 Some words (synonyms) have more or less the same meaning. For example:

disappear · vanish   film · movie   sad · unhappy   small · little
exactly · precisely   more or less · approximately   identical · exactly the same

2 But many related words have similar, but not identical, meanings.

👥 Discuss the difference between . . .

a desk	and	a table
a plant		a tree
similar		identical
a job		a profession
a warm day		a hot day
a big city		a huge city
a cold room		a cool room
a friend		an acquaintance
a friend		a colleague
a funny film		a hilarious film
a laugh		a smile
a scream		a shout
a small village		a tiny village
an accident		a disaster
an interview		a conversation
a discussion		an argument
cross		furious
Don't be silly		Don't be stupid
Don't worry		Don't panic

> *What's the difference between a desk and a table?*
> *— You can sit at either of them.*
> *That's right, yes. But a desk is a special table you use for work or for study.*
> *— Yes and a normal table can be used for different purposes: for eating, or working.*

> *How about a plant and a tree?*
> *— They both have leaves, but a plant is smaller than a tree.*
> *Yes, like an apple tree or a palm tree . . .*

Work

My week

1 Read the article and then answer the questions.

MY WEEK: Gareth Christmas, postman

Gareth Christmas, 65, has been delivering the post in Pontarddulais, South Wales, for 50 years. He will deliver his last letter on New Year's Eve before retiring. — 1

'The post office was a job for life when I first started. I was determined to make a career of it, particularly because of the pension at the end. I started on New Year's Day 1953, so I will have been here for 50 years. My father was a postman before me, and when I was 15 and needed a job he took me with him to the post office in Gorseinon. Of course, I didn't want to work with my father in those days, so I got a job in Pontarddulais, but our branch closed down a few years later and I ended up working with him anyway. — 2

'I've always enjoyed the job; I have a laugh with the boys in the office before I go out, and then I'm my own boss and nobody bothers me. I love being out in the fresh country air and meeting the people. I cover all the farms and drive about 40 to 50 miles a day. I get a lot of breakfasts and cups of tea on my way round, and when I first started I used to come home with bags of vegetables from the farmers. — 3

'The weather does get me down a bit, but you have to take the rough with the smooth, don't you? The summers are nice but the dark winter mornings are the worst, especially when you are up at 4am. — 4

'I was on BBC News yesterday. They filmed me on my round and visiting the local schoolchildren. I often go into the school to give a talk on the post office – the children think it's marvellous, but I haven't managed to persuade any of them to take up my job yet. I do get lots of attention from the kids with this name. A lot of them call me Father Christmas but I have never actually put a red suit on. — 5

'I will really miss the company when I finish, especially the chat in the mornings. But I'm going to be very busy – my daughters want me to do lots of babysitting duty already, so I know that they will definitely be pleased to see more of me. I was supposed to retire at 65 but my birthday was a few weeks ago and I wanted to stay on to make sure I reached 50 years. The wife retires from the civil service around the same time, so it will be nice for us to be at home together. If we start to get on each other's nerves, we will have to go on holiday more often. We already have a few trips arranged. We're off to Tenerife in February and then to Las Vegas in March, so that's a start. — 6

'I haven't really got a leaving party planned but all the boys are meeting up on New Year's Day for a big breakfast and a farewell. I've been here for so many years that I know everybody.' — 7

Sarah X Hall

2 👥 **Write a short answer to each question:**

1 When did Gareth become a postman?
2 Why did Gareth become a postman?
3 What does he not like about his job?
4 Why might his work have made him put on weight?
5 Why does he visit the local school?
6 What will he miss about his work when he retires?
7 Why didn't he retire on his 65th birthday?
8 What is his wife's job and when does she retire?

3 Highlight the phrases in the article which mean the same as these phrases:

¶ 3 share jokes with my colleagues
¶ 4 makes me feel depressed   accept bad times and good times
¶ 6 friendship   annoy each other

4 👥 **Discuss these questions:**

• What would you like and not like about Gareth's job?
• Would you like to work with your father or mother? Why (not)?
• Do you want to be your own boss? Why (not)?
• Do you want to have the same job for 50 years? Why (not)?

A formal letter

Writing

1 👥 Arrange the parts of this letter in the correct order and correct the three spelling mistakes:

```
                                    29 February 2004     1

David Brown
General Manager                                           2
Panorama Hotel
Springfield  SP1 5QY

                              742 Evergreen Terrace       3
                              Springfield  SP8 4UJ

Post of part-time receptionist                           4

Dear Mr Brown,                                           5

I enclose a photograph and a copy of my CV.              6

I am 18 years old and a student at Springfield University,
where I am studying Business and Marketing. I am in good health   7
and am available to work every evening from 6 pm until late.

I could attend an interview at any time convenent to you, but
preferably after 5 pm.                                   8


Jo Miller                                                9
Jo Miller                                                10

Looking forward to hearing from you,                     11

With reference to your advertisement in the 'Springfield
Shopper', I would like to apply for the post of receptionist.     12

Yours sincerly,                                          13
```

2 ✎ **Write a similar application for a part-time job you'd like to have.**

On the road

Traffic in cities

1 👥 **Find the answers to these questions in the text:**

1 When do you have to pay to drive in Central London?
2 How much do you have to pay?
3 How many times can you enter the charging zone in the same day?
4 How do they know your car is in the zone?
5 What if you don't pay the congestion charge?

What is congestion charging?

Congestion charging is a way of ensuring that drivers using valuable and congested road space make a financial contribution.

It encourages the use of other modes of transport and is also intended to ensure that, for those who have to use the roads, journey times are quicker and more reliable.

The London scheme requires drivers to pay £5 per day if they wish to continue driving in central London during the scheme's hours of operation. Payment of the congestion charge allows you to enter, drive around, and leave the charging zone as many times as you wish that day.

There will be no tollbooths or barriers around the congestion charging zone and no physical tickets or passes. Instead, you will be paying to register your vehicle number plate on a database for your journeys within the charging zone.

Cameras will read your registration number as you enter, drive within or leave the congestion charging zone and check it against the database. Once the vehicle number plate has been matched, showing that you have paid, the photographic image of your vehicle will be automatically wiped off the database.

If you have not paid by 10 pm the charge is £10. If you have not paid by midnight you will receive a Penalty Charge Notice of £80. As with parking penalties, this will be reduced to £40 for prompt payment within 14 days. Failure to pay the penalty charge within 28 days will result in the penalty being increased to £120.

2 👥 **Discuss these questions:**

- What are the advantages of the scheme?
- What do you see as the disadvantages?
- Could a similar scheme work in your town or city?
- How safe is it to ride a bike in your city?

🌐 Find out more @
www.tfl.gov.uk

3 👥 **Here are some more ways to reduce traffic problems.**

Which would be best in your town or city?

more	bus lanes
	parking meters
	park & ride schemes
	pedestrian zones
	car parks
	cycle lanes
	roundabouts
	traffic lights
	trams
	buses
	metro lines

Transport

Conjunctions

1 First look at the examples in the Grammar reference section on page 128.

2 👥 Match the sentences that mean the same as each other. Highlight the conjunctions that are used to join the two ideas in each sentence.

After I had bought a magazine, I got on the train.
Even though the train was late I made my connection.
I didn't go by coach because the train was quicker.
The train was late, so I didn't make my connection.
During the time I was on the train I read the magazine.

I didn't make my connection because the train was late.
Before I got on the train I bought a magazine.
I read the magazine while I was on the train.
I went by train because it was faster than the coach.
The train was late but I made my connection.

3 👥 Fill the gaps in these sentences with a suitable conjunction:

1 Many people go by train .... the coach is cheaper.
2 I couldn't buy a bus ticket .... I didn't have any change.
3 The bus finally arrived .... we had been waiting for half an hour.
4 Don't forget to buy a ticket .... you go on the platform.
5 I managed to get a seat on the bus .... it was very full.
6 She first met her boyfriend .... they were both waiting for a bus.

4 👥 Combine these short sentences into single, longer sentences:

1 I forgot to pay the congestion charge. I had to pay £40.   I had ....
2 It was raining quite hard. I didn't get wet.   I didn't ....
3 We were waiting for our plane. We played cards.   We played ....
4 We got on the train. But first we bought some sandwiches.   We bought ....
5 The train left. I realized my bag was still on the rack.   I realized ....
6 The plane ticket was expensive. I went by plane.   I went ....

Looking, seeing, watching

1 👥 Look at definitions 1 and 2. Then match the two halves of definitions 3 to 9:

1 If you **see** something, you notice it with your eyes.
2 If you **look at** something, you try to see it.

3 If you **watch** something,   you see it and are aware of it.
4 If you **stare at** something,   you see it after looking hard for it.
5 If you **peek at** something,   you look at it for a long time.
6 If you **spot** something,   you look for a long time without moving your eyes.
7 If you **notice** something,   you watch it carefully.
8 If you **glance at** something,   you look quickly and secretly.
9 If you **observe** something,   you look for a short time.

2 👥 Fill the gaps in these sentences:
1 I'm .... for my purse – have you .... it?
2 I'm just going to .... at the timetable to .... when the train leaves.
3 I'm .... forward to .... my friends this weekend.
4 It's rude to .... at someone, especially if they .... you're .... at them.
5 I .... the weather forecast on TV and it .... as if it will rain tomorrow.

3 👥 Cover up the photo opposite. Help each other to remember what you could see: how many buses did you see? How many drivers did you notice? etc.

4 👥 You should both look at Activity 42 on page 143. Follow the instructions there.

By land, sea and air

How did you travel?

1 👥 **Look at the photo and discuss these questions:**

- What do/would you enjoy about travelling by ship?
- Do you enjoy long journeys, or do you just want to arrive quickly? Explain why.

2 🔊 **You'll hear the four people in the photo talking about other journeys they have made. Fill in the chart with the information they give:**

	Kim	Rick	Nancy	Andy
How did you travel?	By car			
Why did you choose this method?	Because we had a lot of luggage			
How long did it take?				
What did you enjoy most about the trip?				
Did anything go wrong? If so, what?				

3 👥👥 **Discuss these questions:**

- Which speaker had the worst journey?
- Have you been on any journeys where things went wrong? Tell us about one of them.

EXIT 137
NORTH   UNDECIDED   SOUTH
↓   ↓   ↓

© Mike Baldwin / Cornered

Paragraphs

1 Look at the text below.

Why is the Traffic section easier to read than the Operations section? Highlight the phrase which is the main theme of each paragraph.

Divide the Operations section into paragraphs. Mark the breaks like this: [

Congestion Charging – Summary of Week Two

Traffic

Traffic levels inside the zone remained light throughout the week. Observations indicated traffic was around 20% lower than in a typical working week.

Traffic flowed well, including on the Inner Ring Road, the boundary road of the zone. One significant incident was the diversion into the zone of some traffic on Monday evening after an incident in Grays Inn Road. The procedures laid down for such an incident went very smoothly. Police and traffic managers worked jointly to clear the area and then reopen all routes as quickly as possible.

Bus services ran well all week.

Operations

Almost half a million payments are expected to have been made this week by midnight on Friday 28 February. Payments of the charge for each day throughout the week were: • 93,000 (Monday) • 97,000 (Tuesday) • 99,000 (Wednesday) • 98,000 (Thursday) • Payments for today (Friday) are still being made. In total, around 30,000 Penalty Charge Notices are expected to be issued for the week. Payment channels (text messaging, retail, web and call centre) generally worked well throughout the week although there was an interruption to the web payment facility for a short period late on Thursday evening. A TfL spokesperson said: "The smooth start to the scheme is continuing with traffic levels still well down on a normal working week. The system is working well dealing with many thousands of successful transactions every day."

---

2 Write a report of your experiences of one of these methods of travel:

plane   ship and ferry   car   train   bus or tram   bike

Begin like this: *I love going by . . .* (Use paragraphs to make your report easier to read.)

Requesting and asking permission

1 Listen to two conversations. Which phrases did the speakers use? Which speakers were more polite?

2 Practise saying these phrases:

> I say, could you lend me . . . , please?
> Er, could you lend me . . . ?
> Please will you lend me . . . ?
> Can you lend me . . . ?

YES

> Sure.
> Certainly.
> Of course, here you are.

> Oh, may I borrow your . . . ?
> Can I borrow your . . . ?
> Is it all right if I borrow your . . . ?

NO

> I'm afraid not, because . . .
> No, sorry. You see . . .
> Well, the problem is . . .

3 Note down six things you'd like your partner to do.

Ask each other to do the things on your list.

16-20 Revision

Topic vocabulary

16 There are 25 parts of the body in this puzzle. Can you find them all?

f	d	f	e	n	e	a	t	t	d	e	l	b	o	w	e	e	n	s	e
s	e	e	t	f	n	a	e	o	n	b	n	n	a	f	o	n	n	l	s
h	y	f	h	f	o	a	a	f	n	s	o	u	b	t	t	u	r	i	f
o	e	s	i	l	n	r	r	c	d	g	s	t	g	r	a	b	b	p	b
u	b	t	g	e	n	a	e	a	h	t	u	i	t	e	n	m	a	s	b
l	r	o	h	g	a	f	n	a	w	e	b	e	h	o	r	e	d	c	n
d	o	m	t	h	u	m	b	k	r	r	s	n	r	a	m	n	c	b	k
e	w	a	d	n	s	t	a	n	l	m	i	t	o	b	u	a	s	k	r
r	s	c	n	y	r	b	n	s	s	e	f	s	a	s	c	d	n	e	n
e	d	h	t	n	n	s	t	u	m	m	y	u	t	r	h	n	o	s	e
b	n	a	b	s	n	b	n	l	i	t	t	l	e	f	i	n	g	e	r
a	u	d	n	s	r	t	d	c	h	e	e	k	s	u	n	f	n	e	r

18 Change the British English words to American English in this crossword puzzle:

Across
1 city centre
3 petrol
5 sweets
6 biscuit
7 pavement
9 first floor
11 toilet
12 boot
13 motorway

Down
2 windscreen
4 timetable
6 colour
8 lift
10 CV

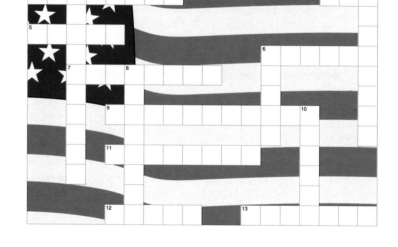

19 There are 23 jobs and professions in this puzzle. Can you find them all?

s	o	c	i	n	i	f	l	i	g	h	t	a	t	t	e	n	d	a	n	t	c	o	n
t	c	h	a	m	b	e	r	m	a	i	d	o	f	a	r	m	e	r	i	p	a	o	p
n	c	b	c	a	s	l	o	c	c	e	c	h	e	f	b	i	c	e	t	i	l	n	n
o	e	f	o	n	i	e	a	s	l	o	i	a	s	o	l	d	i	e	r	l	i	s	c
o	m	w	s	a	p	c	r	e	e	n	s	n	u	r	s	e	c	s	t	o	f	p	n
r	u	a	f	g	o	t	c	a	a	c	n	n	e	w	a	i	t	e	r	t	e	a	j
t	s	i	s	e	s	u	h	m	n	c	u	o	i	c	a	s	h	i	e	r	g	c	b
f	i	t	o	r	t	r	i	a	e	f	i	r	e	f	i	g	h	t	e	r	u	t	t
s	c	r	e	p	m	e	t	n	r	j	s	p	s	s	u	r	g	e	o	n	a	o	j
o	i	e	f	t	a	r	e	i	s	o	c	a	r	e	t	a	k	e	r	n	r	r	b
t	a	s	t	e	n	s	c	c	o	o	t	f	e	b	u	i	l	d	e	r	d	p	i
e	n	s	o	t	u	i	t	f	i	r	e	c	e	p	t	i	o	n	i	s	t	o	o

Grammar review

The numbers (16–20) show the unit where the grammar points were first introduced.

A Fill each gap with a suitable word or phrase:

16 Bob wanted to join .... health club, but .... membership subscription for .... private one near to .... flat was too expensive, so he went to .... public leisure centre in .... town centre, opposite .... station. He enrolled on .... course with .... fitness instructor, but after .... couple of sessions he decided that .... classes were .... waste of time. Then he took .... swimming lessons, which were .... great success. Now he goes to .... pool every day in .... morning before he has .... breakfast.

17 I have tried to solve the puzzles on my own, but in vain. If I .... someone to help me, it .... easier. It .... easier still if someone .... the answer, but ....n't .... so much fun as doing them with a partner.

18 It's such a long time .... we last met. I remember we .... both in London six months ...., so we haven't .... each other .... six months. And you're living in Paris now. How long .... you .... there?

19 Add commas where necessary:

The man.... who has curly hair is Bob.... who has been going out with Sally for six months. Sally.... who used to go out with Bob's brother Tony.... is the sister of Mary.... who used to be Bob's girlfriend!

20 You have to book a ticket .... you travel by air. .... it may be more convenient to book with a travel agent, using the Internet is usually cheaper. Booking early is also a good idea .... it's cheaper than waiting .... there are only a few days left .... you go.

B Rewrite the sentences, using the words in red:

16 Eating a healthy diet can help you to stay healthy.   **food**
If you eat ...., it will help you to .... good health.

17 He felt very frustrated because he couldn't do the word-search puzzle.   **less**
He .... able to do the word-search puzzle.

18 She came to this country four years ago and is still here.   **for**
She .... four years.

19 The traffic was terrible but we weren't delayed.   **even**
We weren't late .... a nightmare.

20 I have a friend called Henry. He is very tall and plays basketball.   **player**
My friend Henry, ... is very tall.

Vocabulary development and pronunciation

16 Put a stress mark on the stressed syllable in these words:

partícularly   accidentally   operation   photography   modern   April   February

17 Which of these do you *make, do* or *take*?

.... a cake .... a shower .... a photo .... a mistake .... your homework

18 What are the British equivalents of these American English terms?

elevator .... pants .... vacation .... ZIP code .... freeway ....

19 Write another word that means the same as these words:

vanish .... unhappy .... more or less .... precisely .... angry ....

20 Fill each gap:

I'm looking .... seeing that film.   I'm looking .... my lost keys.

Can you look .... my cat this weekend?   Look .... that man over there!

Do you remember?

Memories and history

Speaking and vocabulary

1 👥 **Tell each other what you remember about:**

- learning to ride a bike and learning to swim
- your first night away from your mum and dad
- the first time you talked to a stranger in English
- the first time you were home alone
- the first time you travelled to another country

2 👥👥 **Use these phrases to tell each other about your own childhood:**

What happened when you were five years old?
Can you remember something else that happened
when you were five?

When I was five . . .	I probably . . .
When I was six . . .	I remember that I . . .
When I was seven . . .	I think I must have . . .

. . . and continue, year by year, up to last year.

3 👥 **Fill the gaps in these sentences with words from below:**

1 Stonehenge is the most famous .... in Britain. The ring of stones
was built around 2000 .... believe it was a temple.

2 The Parthenon is an .... temple in Athens. It was built between 447 and 432 BC,
became a mosque in the mid fifteenth century and was almost .... by the Venetians in
1687. Recently it has been rebuilt and ....

3 The French .... began in 1789, and France became a .... Napoleon became
.... of France in 1804. In 1812 Napoleon .... Russia with his army, but was
forced to ....

4 In the 19th ...., most of Africa became parts of the British and French ....
After World .... Two these African .... gained their .... and the new
.... became republics.

ancient Archaeologists BC century colonies destroyed Emperor empires
independence invaded monument prehistoric republic restored retreat
Revolution states War

Modal verbs – 2

1 First look at the examples in the Grammar reference section on pages 128 and 129.

2 Match the sentences on the left to the ones with similar meanings on the right.
(**A** is done for you as an example.)

A	She could have won the contest.	=	It was possible for her to win, but she didn't.
	She should have won the contest.	=	She was unlucky not to win.
	She could win the contest.	=	It is possible that she will win.
B	You must have paid a lot of money.		The price was very high.
	You had to pay a lot of money.		You paid too much.
	You shouldn't have paid a lot of money.		The price was probably very high.
C	She can't have done it by herself.		I'm fairly sure she had some help.
	She couldn't do it by herself.		She needed help, but she didn't ask for it.
	She shouldn't have done it by herself.		She was wrong to ask for help.
	She should have done it by herself.		She wasn't able to do it without help.
D	He might have lost your phone number.		He has probably lost it.
	He must have lost your number.		It's impossible that he has lost it.
	He can't have lost your number.		It's possible he has lost it.

3 Fill the gaps in these sentences:

1 You *should have* have asked me for help. I .... helped you.

2 This is very good work, it .... taken you a long time to write.

3 She's going to be very upset, you .... forgotten her birthday.

4 'He's very late – he .... missed the train.'
   'He .... forgotten he was going to meet us.'

5 Nobody .... understand what he was saying, so he .... say it again
   and again.

6 I thought she meant what she said, but she .... serious,
   she .... joking.

4 One of you should look at **Activity 13** on page 134, the other at **Activity 34** on page 140.
You'll be guessing why two people were late for work last week.

Recognizing tones of voice

1 Listen to the recording and match the speakers to their moods:

Alice   Ben   Carl   Donna   Ellie   Frank

angry
confident
disappointed
nervous
sarcastic
sincere

2 Practise saying these sentences in different ways:

1 That's very clever of you! Well done!   sincerely   sarcastically
2 I've got an appointment with the dentist tomorrow.   confidently   nervously
3 You should have asked someone to help you.   sympathetically   angrily
4 Thank you so much for being on time.   pleasantly   sarcastically
5 I wish you'd told me you were going to be late.   unpleasantly   disappointedly

If you're talking to someone on the phone, or you can't see their face, it's sometimes hard to know how they're feeling.

The past

97

A very long time ago

The thrill of history

Sergei Mikhailovich Prokudin-Gorskii: *A Russian Settler's Family*, circa 1910.

1 👥 **Look at the photo and discuss these questions:**

- What do you think life was like for the people in the picture?
- Imagine you are one of them – what happens to you on a typical day?
- What are the differences between your own life and their lives?

2 👥 **Read the text and find the answers to questions 1–5 opposite:**

🌐 Find out more @ www.loc.gov/exhibits/empire + www.dummies.com + www.bbc.co.uk/history + www.historyworld.net

Finding the Bodies: Real Stories, Real People

Two hundred years ago is a long time. Two thousand years ago is impossibly ancient. What do I have in common with anybody who lived back then? How can I be interested in somebody that distant, that strange, and that unreal? 1

They wore funny clothes. They spoke languages nobody speaks anymore. They worshipped cruel gods in flying chariots. They had no computers, no fuel injectors, no freeways and no digital anything except for fingers. They were too worried about survival to watch *Survivor*. Yet they are me. I know it. It's not that I believe in reincarnation and past lives: I don't. Rather, it's that I'm able to reach back through years, decades, centuries, and millennia using great tools – hard evidence and my imagination. 2

If you think of history as lists of facts, dates, battles, and key civilizations, you may discover a lot, but you'll never experience the past's thrill. If, on the other hand, you're able to make the leap – to identify with people who are long dead, to imagine what living their lives must have been like – you may be among those for whom the past becomes a passion, perhaps even an addiction. 3

To do that, you must realize on a gut level that real people walked the earth long ago, and that they carried within them dreams and fears not so unlike yours. It's not so hard, especially with the aid of what the past's people left behind – their cities, art – that shows them looking eerily familiar, and even their exquisitely preserved bodies. 4

Spelling mistakes give your readers a bad impression. Most spelling mistakes are due to slips of the pen or mistyping. Remember to check your spelling before you hand in your work, print it or send it.

1 How many reasons does the writer give that we should **not** be interested in people who lived in the past?

2 Why does he say 'they are me'?

3 Why does he think lists of facts and dates are dull?

4 Why is he passionate about history?

5 What evidence do we have about the lives of people from history?

3 **Highlight** the words in the text which mean the same as these phrases:

¶1 share interests or experiences

¶2 coming back to life in another body   travel in my imagination
solid information   horse-drawn vehicles

¶3 use your imagination   like a drug

¶4 deep down inside yourself   in a strange and frightening way
still in a beautiful condition

Check your spelling

Writing

1 There is a spelling mistake in each line of this text. Cross out the incorrect word and write the correct spelling at the end of the line. The first one has been done for you.

A *myth* is a story. The Greek word '*mythos*' means story. But a myth is a ~~spesial~~ kind of .... *special* 1
story involving gods and goddesses. Long aggo, myths provided people with a view of the 2
world and values to live their lifes by. Stories involving Zeus or Jupiter are myths. 3
Legends are simlar to myths but they are based on history. A legend includes events that 4
may have actually happened to real people. The storys of the Trojan War are legends. 5
Folk tales are traditionall stories which were made up to entertain people. Folk tales 6
involve heroes, heroines, adventures, magical hapenings and sometimes dragons. 7
Fairy tales came out off the Romantic Movement in the 19th century. Writers collected 8
folk tails and published them for literate people to read. 9
History, on the other hand, consists of stories that really hapened in the past. History is 10
not fantasy, but the truth. But different people remember the same events diffrently, and 11
interpret them differently. So how can we know what is the true? 12

2 Look at your three most recent pieces of homework. How many of your spelling mistakes were slips of the pen – mistakes you would have noticed if you had checked your work more carefully?

Your experiences

Speaking and writing

1 Think about two of these topics. Make notes on what you remember.

A personal milestone – an important event that may have changed your life.
An important historical event that you remember happening in your lifetime.
A memorable day – an enjoyable trip, day out or gathering you remember well.

2 Join a partner and find out about each other's experiences.

> I remember very clearly . . .   I can still remember the time . . .
> I'll always remember . . .   Something that I'll never forget is . . .

3 Write a story about a memorable day or event, beginning:

I'll never forget the time . . .

It can be a true story or a made-up, fictitious one. Or even a *partly* true story!

4 Read each other's stories. Can you guess what is true, and what isn't?

Keep up to date

What happened?

Speaking and vocabulary

1 👥 Look at the photos and discuss these questions:

- What do you think is happening in each photo?
- Imagine you are one of the people in each picture. Make up the stories of what happened.

2 👥 How do you react to the news? Read each headline (imagine that they all refer to things that happened in your region) and describe your reaction:

Dog saves children from river

Hundreds homeless after floods

Children save dog from lake

Teachers to get a pay rise

Heavy snow expected on Monday

amused	angry
delighted	depressed
fascinated	horrified
intrigued	not interested
pleased	puzzled
sceptical	upset
shocked	worried

Politicians to get a pay rise

Snow storm stops all traffic

President calls on young people for support

Millionaire, 80, marries model, 18

Serial killer strikes again

Nurses to get a pay rise

- If you only had time to read TWO stories, which would you read? Why?
- Which news interests you? Number these in order of importance for you:

.... local news   .... national news   .... international news

.... sports news   .... business news   .... arts and entertainment news

3 👥👥 Where and when do you find out about the latest news? Ask your partners to do this survey, and tick the appropriate boxes:

	every day	most days	some days	hardly ever	never
TV					
radio					
newspaper					
Internet					
from friends or family					

Prepositions – 2

1 First look at the examples in the Grammar reference section on page 129.

2 👥 Match the endings to the beginnings and add a preposition in the middle:

Everyone praised him ———— *for* ———— his own stupidity.
I find it hard to concentrate   David Beckham.
That story reminds me   the next day's test.
We congratulated him   telling lies and cheating in the exam.
I can't forgive him   doing so well in the exam.
He tried to blame us   his performance in the concert.
They named their son   a funny thing that happened to me.
I spent all evening preparing   speaking to me so rudely.
He punished his son   my homework with the TV on.

3 👥 Fill each gap with a suitable preposition:

A woman came home [____] work and found her husband [____] the kitchen. She was terrified because he was shaking all over [____] what looked like a wire running [____] his waist [____] the electric kettle. She wanted to get him away [____] the deadly current, so she hit him [____] a large piece [____] wood that was lying [____] the back door, and broke his arm [____] two places. This was a pity because the man had only been listening [____] his Walkman.

Spelling and pronunciation   Pronunciation and vocabulary development

1 👥 The words in red are spelt the same but pronounced differently. Read these sentences aloud, then listen to the recording.

1 Please close the door.   Don't sit so close to me.
2 This is a valuable object.   I object to being spoken to like that.
3 Have you read the news?   Did you read the news?
4 How do I record my voice?   She set a new Olympic record.
5 They had a terrible row.   Everyone was sitting in a row.
6 Careful not to tear your dress.   There were tears in his eyes.
7 I used to play cards a lot.   Sand is used to make glass.
8 The wind is very cold.   How do I wind the tape back?

2 👥 The words in the lists are spelt differently but pronounced the same. You certainly know almost all of these words, but there may be a few you're unsure about. If so, see if your partner knows the difference (see the example below).

Highlight ONLY the words you are unsure of.

board · bored	higher · hire	right · write	threw · through
buy · by · bye	hole · whole	scene · seen	to · too · two
cent · sent · scent	knew · new	sea · see	waist · waste
eye · I	mail · male	son · sun	wait · weight
find · fined	nose · knows	stair · stare	war · wore
flour · flower	one · won	steal · steel	warn · worn
guessed · guest	passed · past	tail · tale	way · weigh
hear · here	peace · piece	their · there · they're	weak · week

What's the difference between
R O O T and R O U T E?

— A root is the part of a plant that's under the ground.
A route is the way you get somewhere.

The news

101

Here is the news . . .

Listening

1 🔊 Listen to the news broadcast and match the headlines to the places they happened:

'Help, we are being kidnapped!'

Homeless – thanks to the cat

Moldovans snorkel to new life

Teacher nearly killed by books

'Twice is enough'

Amsterdam, Holland
Austria
Calgary, Canada
Germany
Zagreb, Croatia

2 🔊 Listen again and fill the gaps in each summary:

1 The women's team from Moldova were ...*missing*... from the World Underwater Hockey Championships in Calgary. They obtained Canadian .... as members of an international .... team, by paying $................. to a people-smuggler. They have all disappeared.

2 A teacher in Zagreb, Croatia, had a lucky escape after his .... heard strange .... coming from his flat. The police found the .... -year-old .... teacher in bed. He couldn't .... after the books had fallen on him.

3 Two young Austrian .... were in a car driven by their .... As a joke they put a .... in the window: 'Help, we are being kidnapped!' The police stopped the car and .... the aunt. Later the aunt was .... – she was not ....

4 A former university lecturer in Amsterdam, Holland, doesn't want Dutch people to give each other .... kisses when they say hello. He says the habit is useless and that .... are often upset – especially when the third kiss is on the ....! He has given away .... badges saying: 'Twice is enough'. People who wear the badges are showing they only want to be kissed ....

5 Elsie and Walter Kochentopf's cat, Robbie, accidentally turned on the .... tap while they were watching TV. Water was dripping from the .... and flowing down the .... They removed everything from the cellar, but forgot that their .... was cooking in the kitchen. A .... started which .... the kitchen and hallway. They are now homeless while their house is being ....

🌐 Read the news @
news.bbc.co.uk +
www.guardian.co.uk +
news.yahoo.com +
news.google.co.uk

The news

Writing a report

1 👥 Look at this advice about how to write a report. Fill the gaps with suitable words from the list on the right:

1 A report is a description of an .... or situation. As with any writing, a good report should be written with your .... in mind. Think about how they will react to what you are telling them.

2 Before you start writing, note down all the main .... you want to make – and arrange them in the right .... If there is a word-limit for the report, you may have to leave out some .... – so decide what to leave out before you start writing. If possible, include some .... – knowing what some people involved said will help to bring your report to ....

3 Remember that first impressions and last impressions are important. A good first sentence helps to set the .... and arouse the reader's .... A good last sentence leaves the reader feeling better .... or even .... after reading your report.

details
direct
speech
event
impressed
informed
interest
life
order
points
readers
scene

2 🔊 Listen to this news story and make notes as you listen.

> **They wanted to win £1 million**

3 ✎ Write the story in your own words.

I read in the paper . . .

1 👥 One of you should look at **Activity 15** on page 135, the other at **Activity 35** on page 140. Find out the story behind one of these headlines and then tell your partner about it.

> ATM Gives Out Free Cash

> **Police Use Special Cars to Catch Car Thieves**

> I read a good story in the paper today.
> Did you read about . . . ?
> Did you hear about . . . ?

> Tell me about it.
> Tell me more!
> What happened next?

2 ✎ Find an interesting or amusing story in a newspaper printed in your language. Rewrite the report in your own words (in English!). Follow the advice above.

👥 Read each other's stories.

'Why can't the newspapers run more good-news stories?'

23A Reading for pleasure

What do you read?

1 👥 **Discuss these questions:**

- Which of the magazines above might you be interested in? Why?
- What were the last two magazines you bought? And the last two books?
- How much time do you spend reading for pleasure in an average week?
- How long do you spend reading for your studies (or work) each week?

2 👥 **Think about what you read in your own language. Number the reading matter to show how often you read them: 0 = never, 1 = hardly ever, 2 = from time to time, 3 = frequently, 4 = very often, 5 = every day.**

advertisements	....	letters	....	recipes	....
CD inserts and covers	....	literature	....	reports	....
comic books	....	magazines	....	reviews	....
e-mails	....	newspapers	....	textbooks	....
fiction	....	non-fiction	....	thrillers	....
instructions	....	official forms	....	websites	....

Now think about the future: what will you need to read in English? Number the items above in order of importance (0 = not important at all, 10 = very important).

3 👥 **In which department of a bookshop would you find these titles?**

TITLE	DEPARTMENT
10 Best Sherlock Holmes Stories	Audio books
100 Wonderful English Recipes	Biography
1000 Great Inventions	Children's
A Complete Atlas of the World	Cookery
Basketball Skills and Drills	Crime
Eyewitness Guide to the Greek Islands	Health
Great Expectations by Charles Dickens	History
Harry Potter and the Chamber of Secrets read by Stephen Fry	Literature
Help Yourself to a Better Memory	Reference
The Friendly Dragon	Science and technology
The Invisible Man	Science fiction
The Life of Charles Dickens	Self-help
The New Book of Vitamins	Sports
The Second World War	Travel

- What kinds of books do you read?
- What were the titles of the last three books you read? Which did you enjoy most and why?

Books

–ing and *to . . .* – 2

1 First look at the examples in the Grammar reference section on page 124.

2 👥 Complete the sentences with your own ideas:

1 Can you run for half an hour without *stopping for a rest* ?
2 Can you write a letter in English without .... ?
3 Can you sneeze without .... ?
4 Can you stop hiccups by .... ?
5 Can you touch your toes without .... ?
6 Can you keep your eyes open for a whole minute without .... ?
7 Can you stay awake all night without .... ?

3 👥 Match the beginnings to the endings:

1	I can't afford	complaining about everything.
2	I gave up	laughing when I saw her new hairstyle.
3	I couldn't help	not to notice when he shouted at me.
4	Will you please help me	to make the phone call for me.
5	She keeps on	to go out every night.
6	I'd like you	to go with him to the concert.
7	I don't mind	to see a film rather than go out for a meal?
8	He persuaded me	to translate this report?
9	Would you prefer	trying to phone him after getting no answer.
10	I pretended	waiting for you if you're not quite ready.

Two-word words

Some two-word words are written as two separate words, like *soap opera* and *game show*. Some are written as one word, like *newspaper* and *textbook*. Most two-word adjectives are usually written with a hyphen, like *short-sighted* and *brand-new*.

1 👥 Match these words to form two-word nouns. Then decide which are written as one word (like *motorway*) and which as two words (like *main road*):

2 👥 Match these words to make two-word adjectives:

24-................. 	absent-................. 	all-................. 	all-................. 	brand- ....

first-................. 	home-................. 	kind-................. 	left-................. 	long- ....

old-................. 	one-................. 	self-................. 	short-................. 	well- ....

class   day   fashioned   handed   hearted   hour   known   lost   made
minded   new   night   service   sighted   way

Books

Chapter 1

Chapter 1 *Only me, Jojo*

It's dark again. So it's evening. It's the third evening. No, I'm wrong. It's the fourth evening.

It's . . . Tuesday . . . Wednesday . . . Thursday. Yes, it's Thursday. Why do I count the days? Why do I say it's Thursday? There aren't any more days. There's just time. Time when it's dark, and time when it's light.

Everything is dead, so why not days, too? Yes. No more days. No more Thursdays. There's only now.

And there's only me. Why? Why aren't I dead, too?

That's a stupid question, Jojo, I say to myself. You know why you aren't dead. You aren't dead because you weren't in the house. You were in the fields when the men came. But that's not my question. I want to know why I was in the fields. Why wasn't I in the house with my family?

There are no answers to questions like that, Jojo, I tell myself. I have to talk to myself because there isn't anyone else. I think there are mice here. I can hear them at night. You can't talk to mice. But there aren't any other people. There's only me. Jojo.

I know this because I listen. I listen all day and all night. I hide in our stable, where the horse lived. And I hear nothing. Just the mice. The village is quiet. There is smoke now, but smoke is quiet. The fires were noisy, but the fires have stopped. It rained yesterday, and after the rain there were no more fires. Just smoke.

from *Jojo's Story* by Antoinette Moses

🔊 👥 **Listen to the three extracts and then discuss these questions:**

- Which story would you like to read more of? Why?
- How do you think each story will develop? What might happen next?
- Do you like audio books? Or do you prefer to read in the normal way? Why?

Chapter 1 *Summer in the city*

They say if you don't like the heat, get out of the kitchen. New York, mid-July, if you don't like the heat, get out of the city. Anyone who could take a vacation was in the mountains or on Long Island. Anywhere cooler than the city. But me, I had work to do and dollars to earn. As I left my apartment building in Queens, the heat hit me. The temperature was already up in the eighties. Only seven o'clock in the morning and I was sweating. It was going to be another one of those hot, uncomfortable days. Time to catch the number seven train to Manhattan.

The name's Marley, Nat Marley. I know the city of New York like the back of my hand. New York is part of me, it's in my blood. During my fifteen years' service with the New York Police Department, I saw the best and worst of life in the city. After leaving the NYPD, I became a private investigator. Although I don't make that much money, I'm my own boss and I don't have to take orders from anybody. I prefer it that way.

At Grand Central Station, crowds of office workers hurried out to 42nd Street. There were usually a few homeless people in the station trying to make a few dollars before the police moved them along. When you make the same trip every day, you get to know people's faces. But today, I couldn't see any homeless people. Maybe they were out in the sunshine on 42nd Street.

from *High Life, Low Life* by Alan Battersby

CHAPTER
One

If you are interested in stories with happy endings, you would be better off reading some other book. In this book, not only is there no happy ending, there is no happy beginning and very few happy things in the middle. This is because not very many happy things happened in the lives of the three Baudelaire youngsters. Violet, Klaus and Sunny Baudelaire were intelligent children, and they were charming and resourceful, and had pleasant facial features, but they were extremely unlucky, and most everything that happened to them was rife with misfortune, misery and despair. I'm sorry to tell you this, but that is how the story goes.

from *The Bad Beginning* by Lemony Snicket.

Sporting mistakes – 2

👥 Here are two reviews by young readers of *The Bad Beginning* from a bookstore website. Correct the writers' mistakes (spelling, punctuation and use of capital letters):

The Bad Beginning – a great read!

A series of unfortunate events aren't like normal books. The children's misfortune begins when their parents are killed when their house is burnt down. Even though they have a lot of bad luck, I thought the books were amazing. I am on the third one now and all of them so far have been really excellent. It's a real page-turner, the bad beginning, and it's sequal. I would recommend these books to anyone of any age. It didn't matter to me that there was no Happy Ending, it's really the story that counts and how the author writes it.

Lemony Snicket, the new J.K. Rowling?

I am a child and thought that all you bookworms out there would like to read a review from a young persons point of view. This enchanting book was so good I literally couldn't put it down. Lemony Snicket can make you laugh and cry at the same time. The Bad Beginning is about three little children Violet (the oldest), then Klaus and baby Sunny. They soon unfortunatley find out from one of their parents closet friends that thier beloved mother and father have died in a fire in thier own home. They are sent to live with a long-lost relative called Count Olaf. Even form his name you can gess that he is most proberbly is very unkind and frighting. The three orphans still have lots of missfortune to come in this book and the rest of the seris to come. I definatly advice you to read this book if you want to be in a dreamland of imagination.

👁 Readers notice mistakes in writing more than listeners notice mistakes in speech.
On the Internet people are much more tolerant of mistakes than examiners (or teachers?). In e-mails to friends or colleagues mistakes matter even less.

Check your answers in **Activity 37** on page 141.

A really good book!

1 👥👥 **What are some good books you've read lately? Tell your partners about them. Mention some of these points:**

- your expectations before starting
- other books by the same author
- kind of book, how long it took you to read it
- the content (and, if it was a novel, the characters)
- the style of writing
- your feelings after finishing
- why your friends would enjoy it

2 ✎ **Write a review of a book, recommending it to a friend and explaining why he or she would enjoy it. (If you never read books, you could write about a film – but not the same one you wrote about in Unit 8.)**

3 👥 **Show your completed work to a partner, and read your partner's work.**

🌐 Find out more @
uk.cambridge.org/elt/readers +
www.lemonysnicket.com
And www.amazon.com lets you 'look inside' many popular books and read the first chapter.

Books

107

24A Friends

Good friends

1 👥 The photos show friends talking together. Discuss these questions and decide on your stories:

- What is the 'story' behind each picture?
- What are the people saying to each other?
- What happened **before** and what happened **afterwards**?

👥 + 👥 Join another pair and tell each other your stories.

2 👥 Discuss these questions:

- Which of the following things would you expect your friends to do for you?
- Which of those things would **you** do for your friends?
- What else do real friends do for each other?

take the blame for something you did	travel across the city to see you
tell you all his or her secrets	lend you money
pay for you in a restaurant	let you win a game against him or her
listen to your troubles	remember your birthday
phone you every day	give you advice
tell the truth, even if it hurts you	send you flowers
keep a secret	not talk about you behind your back
not hold a grudge	help with your problems

3 👥👥 Ask your partners these questions:

- Why are friends important to **you**?
- Who is your **oldest** friend?
  How did you first meet? Why did you become friends?
- Who is your **newest** friend?
  How did you meet and why did you become friends?
- What are some reasons why you might stop being friends with someone?

> My best friend is . . . We first met in . . .
> We get on so well because . . .
> We have so much in common. For example, . . .

Two-word verbs

1 First look at the examples in the Grammar reference section on pages 129 and 130.

2 Any of the verbs on the left can be combined with any of the words on the right to make two-word verbs:

come drive get go fall move ride run walk		away back down in off on
bring carry drive get lift move pull push take	something	out over past round up

👥 Write six sentences with a gap for a two-word verb. Here are two examples to start you off:

Do _____ and see us again soon. (come back)
I want to watch that DVD again. When are you going to _____ ? (bring it back)

Exchange sentences with another pair – can you fill all the gaps?

3 👥 Which of these sentences are wrong?

a Someone has taken my glass away. **d** Someone has taken away my glass.
b Someone has taken it away. **e** Someone has taken away it.
c Someone has it away taken. **f** My glass has been taken away.

Tick the correct sentences and put a cross by the wrong ones:

1	He wrote down his name. ✓	He wrote down it. ✗
2	He jumped off the cliff.	He jumped the cliff off.
3	She opened up the parcel.	She opened up it.
4	I had to look after my brother.	I had to look after him.
5	I was looking for my keys.	I was looking them for.
6	Flowers come in the spring out.	Flowers come out in the spring.
7	She walked past the open shop.	The shop was open but she walked past.
8	He gave away all his money.	He gave all his money away.

4 Replace the words in red with a word or phrase that means the same:

1 What time is the news on?   *being broadcast*
2 The lesson is over, it's time to be off.
3 The match is off because of the rain.
4 The film won't be out on DVD for 6 months.
5 Have you been up for long?
6 I'll be out till 7, after that I'll be in all evening.
7 I'll be back soon.
8 What's up? Is my time up already?

5 Rewrite each sentence, replacing the words in green with a two-word verb from below:

1 The plane left on time.   *The plane took off on time.*
2 Please remove your shoes when you enter.
3 Just relax in your chair, don't continue worrying.
4 Please wait a moment, I want to show you these old photos I've found.
5 If you want to lose weight you must stop eating sweets and start swimming.
6 I used to like Mary but now I've stopped liking her.
7 I asked you to reduce the volume on the radio, not press the off button.
8 When you register at a hotel you have to complete a form.

check in   come across   fill in/out   get on with   give up   go in
go off   hold on   keep on   sit back   ~~take off~~   take up   turn down   turn off   take off

People

109

Men and women, boys and girls

Who's who?

1 👥 Match these words to the people in the pictures.

adventurous	confident	funny	quiet	serious
aggressive	considerate	imaginative	reliable	shy
amusing	conventional	kind	reserved	sociable
arrogant	easy-going	lively	self-satisfied	talkative
calm	fashionable	modest	sensible	tolerant
cheerful	friendly	practical	sensitive	unfriendly

2 🔊 Now you'll hear each of these people being described by a friend or colleague. Identify each person and write their name below their picture. Then discuss these questions:

- Did your judgement of their personality match their friends' descriptions?
- Which of them would you like to get to know, and why?

3 👥 Take turns to describe each person in your own words. Your partner must guess who you're talking about – but not until you've spoken for at least 30 seconds.

People

Describing people

> *What does she look like?*
> *How can I recognize him?*

> — *She's sixteen but she looks older . . .*
> — *He's quite tall and slim . . .*

1 👥 Add two more words or phrases to each list, using a dictionary if necessary:

Age	eighteen twentyish middle-aged
Height	medium-height tall
Build	slim muscular
Hair colour	dark fair
Hairstyle	wavy straight bald balding
Eyes	brown
Appearance	good-looking handsome
Clothes	smart scruffy casual
	jeans suit t-shirt

👥 + 👥 Compare your lists.

2 👥 Describe what the people in the photos opposite look like. You can't actually see their bodies or clothes, but can you guess what they're wearing and how they look?

3 👤 Note down a few words to describe the following people:

One of your male relations
A favourite female film star
A favourite teacher
A person who is in the news

One of your female relations
A favourite male film star
A member of your class
Another member of your class

👥 Describe each person to your partner, but don't say who it is. Your partner must guess!

4 👥 One of you should look at **Activity 16** on page 135, the other at **Activity 36** on page 141. You'll see more people to describe to each other.

5 ✎ An English friend has offered to meet your two best friends when they arrive at the airport in London, but he has never met them. Reply to his e-mail:

> How can I recognize your friends at the airport?
> What do they look like?

25A A sense of humour

I don't get it!

'Surf's up!'

1 👥 **Compare your reactions to the cartoons and then discuss these questions:**

> If you drop a white hat into the Red Sea, what does it become?
> — Wet.

- Why are penguins funny? What other animals are funny too?
- Look back at all the previous cartoons in this book. Which make you smile? Which do you NOT find funny? Why?
- What sort of things make you laugh?
- What is the funniest movie you've seen? Why was it so funny?
- Who is the most famous comedian in your country? Why is he or she so popular?

2 👥 **Different things are considered funny in different cultures. Which of these do you think are funny?**

> What do you call a boomerang that won't come back?
> — A stick.

I'm on a sea food diet. I see food. I eat it.

You look well!

> | I don't get it. | I can't see the funny side of... |
> | I think that's in bad taste. | That just isn't funny. |
> | It doesn't appeal to me. | It's all a matter of taste. |

3 👥 **One of you should look at Activity 18 on page 136, the other at Activity 38 on page 142. You each have one sharp and one blurred picture. Ask questions to find out about the blurred pictures.**

Adverbs and word order
Grammar practice

1 First look at the examples in the Grammar reference section on page 130.

2 👥 These sentences look funny because the adverbs are in the wrong place. Put them in the correct places:

What do you call a pig with three eyes?
— A piiig.

1 I laugh never at practical jokes.
2 Whenever I tell a joke I forget the punch line always.
3 When an adverb is put in the wrong place it looks funny often.
4 He slipped and fell unexpectedly over.
5 I yesterday saw a very funny film.
6 She gets hardly ever the jokes I tell.
7 I like very much funny films.
8 I'm tonight going to the cinema with my friends.
9 Everyone loudly laughed when he fell into the swimming pool.
10 Enough funnily, I've already seen that film.

3 👥 Place each adverb in the best place in each sentence:

Why is the letter T like an island?
— Because it's in the middle of 'waTer'.

1	I'm going to Greece this summer.	probably
2	He's leaving the country.	soon
3	She plays the piano.	very well
4	We all laughed when he spilt his coffee.	heartily
5	I could understand what he was saying.	hardly
6	I had my mobile phone with me.	luckily
7	Have you ridden a motorbike?	ever
8	He didn't get the joke.	obviously
9	As the door opened I put away the chocolates.	slowly quickly
10	He told me he was going to phone me.	yesterday today

Reading aloud
Pronunciation

If someone asks you to read something aloud to them, such as a couple of sentences from a newspaper or book, you need to be able to read clearly and confidently.

1 🔊 👥 Read these jokes aloud, with one of you as the doctor and the other as the patient. Then listen to the model versions:

Why is U a happy letter?
— Because it's in the middle of 'fun'.

Doctor, doctor, I think I'm a computer!
— How long have you felt like this?
Ever since I was switched on!

Doctor, doctor, my little brother thinks he's a computer.
— Well, bring him in so I can cure him.
I can't, I need to use him to finish my homework!

Doctor, doctor, my computer screen is giving me a headache.
— Why's that?
I keep banging my head on it!

2 👥 + 👥 Two of you should look at Activity 19 on page 136, the others at Activity 41 on page 142. Rehearse your jokes, then perform your jokes to each other!

That's funny!

Topic vocabulary

21 There are 21 words from Unit 21 in this puzzle. Can you find them all?

```
h  y  a  r  c  h  a  e  o  l  o  g  i  s  t  i  h  y
t  o  w  o  r  l  d  w  a  r  t  w  o  o  a  r  m  y
o  t  h  e  p  a  s  t  a  n  c  i  e  n  t  g  m  t
h  s  h  p  c  e  n  t  u  r  y  o  p  i  n  t  o  t
o  t  e  m  p  l  e  r  e  p  u  b  l  i  c  i  n  c
i  n  d  e  p  e  n  d  e  n  c  e  k  o  o  t  u  o
r  t  t  r  e  t  r  e  a  t  s  m  y  t  h  a  m  l
t  t  t  h  t  y  y  h  m  i  l  e  s  t  o  n  e  o
t  s  s  l  c  h  i  l  d  h  o  o  d  y  t  y  n  n
y  l  e  g  e  n  d  h  i  s  t  o  r  i  a  n  t  y
o  y  r  c  i  v  i  l  i  z  a  t  i  o  n  i  t  s
y  r  e  s  t  o  r  e  r  a  a  e  m  p  i  r  e  y
```

23 Try this crossword puzzle:

Across

1   This encourages you to buy something
4   The works of Shakespeare, for example
8   A book about someone's life
10 'Superman', for example
12 A person who writes books
13 An article about a book or film
14 They tell you how to operate something

Down

2   Books about history or science
3   You're reading one now!
5   An exciting story
6   They're published every day
7   A place on the Internet
9   How to cook something
11 Read the words of the songs on a CD here

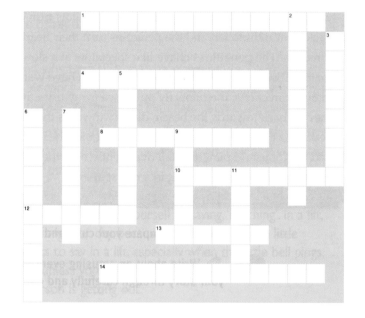

24 There are 24 adjectives you can use to describe people in this puzzle. Can you find them all?

```
e  c  x  g  l  e  x  v  g  l  u  a  d  v  e  n  t  u  r  o  u  s
g  f  o  i  m  a  g  i  n  a  t  i  v  e  k  i  n  d  v  u  c  g
a  o  a  n  e  c  o  n  v  e  n  t  i  o  n  a  l  e  l  u  h  c
r  m  o  s  s  h  y  o  g  r  p  r  a  c  t  i  c  a  l  s  e  o
r  h  u  d  h  i  s  e  y  e  g  o  y  s  e  n  s  i  b  l  e  n
o  a  t  s  l  i  d  c  u  o  g  g  t  o  l  e  r  a  n  t  r  f
g  n  a  e  c  o  o  e  r  o  v  l  a  m  u  s  i  n  g  x  f  i
a  d  l  u  r  u  o  n  r  u  y  y  g  o  e  o  o  o  e  s  x  u  d
n  s  l  e  l  r  l  k  a  a  f  x  e  d  r  e  l  i  a  b  l  e
t  o  l  g  y  r  l  a  i  b  t  f  s  e  n  s  i  t  i  v  e  n
r  m  y  i  v  s  v  o  r  n  l  e  y  s  o  q  u  i  e  t  v  t
o  e  y  l  m  r  v  g  y  o  g  e  e  t  r  e  s  e  r  v  e  d
```

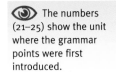

Grammar review

A Fill each gap with a suitable word or phrase:

21 'Why are they so late?'

'They .... got lost – or they .... delayed in the traffic, perhaps?'

'No, they .... forgotten to come!'

22 .... midnight .... January 30th, two men who stole bicycles .... a shop .... Newcastle were arrested .... the police followed their tyre tracks .... the snow .... their front door.

23 You turn the TV on ......press...... this button. But ......set...... the video is a bit more complicated. Would you like me ......explain...... to you how to do it? Or would you prefer ......find out...... how to do it ......read...... the instruction book?

24 He said he was .... and walked .... slowly – but a few minutes later he was .... again.

'What's .... ?' I asked.

'I was looking .... my keys,' he said.

'Oh sorry, I forgot to give them .... to you. It's a good job you came .... now. You're lucky to catch me ...., I was just going ....'

Rewrite the sentences, using the words in red:

B **21** Silly girl! She didn't send her grandfather a birthday card.   remembered

She .... to send her grandfather a birthday card.

22 The police said that the accident was his fault.   blamed

The police .... the accident.

23 It's impossible to sneeze and keep your eyes open at the same time.   without

Nobody can .... eyes at the same time.

24 Someone has removed my bag – who did it?   away

Who has ....?

25 My guess is that he didn't get the joke.   probably

He .... the joke.

Vocabulary development and pronunciation

21 Write a suitable adverb to show how these sentences might be spoken:

'You did that <u>very</u> well!' he said ....

'You complete idiot!' she shouted ....

'I have a job interview tomorrow,' he said ....

'Thank you so much for waiting,' she said ....

22 Correct the 15 spelling mistakes – a spell-checker wouldn't find any of them!

This weak I red in the paper about too workers who were scent to prison for steeling there boss's car, a couple who gave a read flour to every guessed at they're wedding, and won article about the write weigh to reduce your waste line and lose wait.

23 Match the words in blue to the ones in red to make two-word words:

absent- brand- first- full kind- left- police old- reading

class fashioned handed hearted list minded new station stop

24 Replace the verbs in green with two-word verbs:

He entered the flat, removed his shoes, relaxed on the sofa, and pressed the 'on' switch of the TV.

25 Write the punch lines to these jokes:

'Doctor, I think I'm a dog.' ' ....,'

'Doctor, everyone keeps ignoring me.' ' ....,'

'Doctor, doctor, I keep thinking there are two of me.' 'One ....,'

Grammar reference

Index

Irregular verbs

verb · past simple · past participle

be · was/were · been
bear · bore · born
beat · beat · beaten
become · became · become
begin · began · begun
bend · bent · bent
bite · bit · bitten
blow · blew · blown
break · broke · broken
bring · brought · brought
build · built · built
burst · burst · burst
buy · bought · bought
catch · caught · caught
choose · chose · chosen
come · came · come
cost · cost · cost
cut · cut · cut
dig · dug · dug
draw · drew · drawn
drink · drank · drunk
drive · drove · driven
eat · ate · eaten
fall · fell · fallen
feed · fed · fed
feel · felt · felt
fight · fought · fought
find · found · found
flee · fled · fled
fly · flew · flown
forget · forgot · forgotten
forgive · forgave · forgiven
freeze · froze · frozen
get · got · got (US gotten)
give · gave · given

go · went · gone/been
grow · grew · grown
hang · hung · hung
have · had · had
hear · heard · heard
hide · hid · hidden
hit · hit · hit
hold · held · held
hurt · hurt · hurt
keep · kept · kept
know · knew · known
lay · laid · laid
lead · led · led
leave · left · left
lend · lent · lent
let · let · let
lie · lay · lain
(lie · lied · lied = not tell the truth)
light · lit · lit
lose · lost · lost
make · made · made
mean · meant · meant
meet · met · met
pay · paid · paid
put · put · put
read · read · read /ri:d red red/
ride · rode · ridden
ring · rang · rung
rise · rose · risen
run · ran · run
say · said · said
see · saw · seen
sell · sold · sold
send · sent · sent
set · set · set

shake · shook · shaken
shine · shone · shone
shoot · shot · shot
show · showed · shown
shut · shut · shut
sing · sang · sung
sink · sank · sunk
sit · sat · sat
sleep · slept · slept
slide · slid · slid
speak · spoke · spoken
spend · spent · spent
spread · spread · spread
stand · stood · stood
steal · stole · stolen
stick · stuck · stuck
sting · stung · stung
strike · struck · struck
swear · swore · sworn
sweep · swept · swept
swim · swam · swum
swing · swung · swung
take · took · taken
teach · taught · taught
tear · tore · torn
tell · told · told
think · thought · thought
throw · threw · thrown
tread · trod · trod
understand · understood · understood
wake · woke · woken
wear · wore · worn
weep · wept · wept
win · won · won
write · wrote · written

1 Present simple and past simple

1. We use the **present simple** to talk about general truths, and unchanging or regular events or actions:

   ✓ Water freezes at 0° Celsius.   ✗ Water is freezing at 0° Celsius.

   ✓ In the UK children start school at age five.   ✗ In the UK children are starting school at age five.

   ✓ I always have sugar in my coffee.   ✗ I am always having sugar in my coffee.

   ✓ I never watch scary movies.   ✗ I am never watching scary movies.

   ✓ When do you usually get up?   ✗ When are you usually getting up?

2. We often use these **adverbs** with the **present simple**:

   always   usually   often   generally   normally   never   hardly ever   sometimes

   ✓ Our football team generally loses.   ✗ Our football team loses generally.

   ✓ We hardly ever win.   ✗ We win hardly ever.

3. We use the **past simple** to talk about events that happened at a particular time in the past:

   ✓ He flew to Spain last Sunday.   ✗ He has flown to Spain last Sunday.

   ✓ She started school when she was four years old.   ✗ She has started school when she was four years old.

   ✓ I didn't know she was married until she told me.   ✗ I haven't known she was married until she told me.

4. We often use these **adverbs** and **adverbial phrases** with the **past simple**:

   after that   in 1999   last Sunday   last week   last year   next   then

   I went to London last year.

5. We use the **past simple** after *When . . . ?* or *What time . . . ?* when referring to the past:

   ✓ When did you hear the news?   ✗ When have you heard the news?

   ✓ What time did you get up today?   ✗ What time have you got up today?

6. **Regular verbs**

present	He enjoys parties.	He doesn't enjoy parties.	Does he enjoy parties?
past	She enjoyed the party.	She didn't enjoy the party.	Did she enjoy the party?
present perfect	We've enjoyed the party.	We haven't enjoyed the party.	Have you enjoyed the party?
passive	The party was enjoyed **by** everyone.	The party wasn't enjoyed by everyone.	Was the party enjoyed by everyone?

   Pronunciation of regular verbs:

   –s may be pronounced /s/ or /z/ or /ɪz/:   likes /laɪks/ enjoys /ɪndʒɔɪz / watches /wɒtʃɪz/

   –ed may be pronounced /t/ or /d/ or /ɪd/:   liked /laɪkt/ enjoyed /ɪndʒɔɪd/ started /stɑːtɪd/

7. **Irregular verbs**

present	He eats cakes.	He doesn't eat cakes.	Does he eat cakes?
past	She ate the cakes.	She didn't eat the cakes.	Did she eat the cakes?
present perfect	We've eaten the cakes.	We haven't eaten the cakes.	Have you eaten the cakes?
passive	The cakes were eaten.	The cakes weren't eaten.	Were the cakes eaten?

2a Prepositions – 1

1. Prepositions of **place**:

   in   on   at   behind   in front of   beside   between   among   under   underneath
   on top of   inside   outside   near to   a long way from   on the right of   etc.

   The missing wallet was underneath a pile of books behind the desk in my bedroom.

2. Prepositions of **motion** and **direction**:

   into   on to   past   through   over   under   down from   etc.

   They ran through the field and jumped over the fence.

   Are you going past the post office when you come back from the bank?

3. Prepositions of **time**:

   at   in   on   before   after   during   past   etc.

   It happened on Tuesday at ten past eight in the morning, after breakfast.

4 Some prepositions are part of **fixed phrases**:

in fact   at the moment   in search of   for the first time   at the bottom of   in general   etc.

5 *by* is used with the **passive**:

Macbeth was written by Shakespeare.

2b Punctuation

1 We use an **apostrophe** to write contractions:

it's   it isn't   I haven't   he's arrived

and to make the possessive form of nouns:

the cat's basket   John's book   his two sisters' rooms

2 We use a **comma** to separate parts of a sentence that don't identify the subject:

My mother, who is 82, doesn't eat sweets.

but not when one part does identify the other:

The lady who owns the shop is 82.

We also use **commas** to separate items in a list:

a tall, dark, handsome man   we need eggs, fish, milk and butter

and before question-tags and forms of address:

It's nice, isn't it?   Thanks, John.   Good morning, sir.

We often use **commas** to separate an adverbial clause from a main clause:

If it's fine tomorrow, we can go out.

but not usually when the main clause comes first:

We can go out if it's fine tomorrow.

3 We use single or double **inverted commas** to quote speech, and in titles:

'That's right,' he said.   He said, "That's right."

"Lord Of The Rings" was very exciting.

4 We use **capital letters** at the beginning of sentences, and at the beginning of days of the week, months, public festivals, nationalities, languages, names of people and their titles:

Monday   July   Christmas   British   English   Leo Jones   Uncle John

We also use **CAPITALS** in some abbreviations:

BBC   HQ   UK   USA

but not in others:

e.g.   etc.   i.e.   approx.   max.   min.

5 Here are more common punctuation marks:

full stop.   question mark?   exclamation mark!   colon: hyphen -   dash –   (brackets)

---

3 and 16 Articles and quantifiers

1 Some nouns are '**countable**':

banana   bottle   car   child/children   fact   hour   job   person/people   piece   slice   etc.

How many cars can you see?   That is an interesting fact.

Some cars are faster than others.   I love bananas.

Other nouns are '**uncountable**':

beer   bread   fruit   information   traffic   time   work   etc.

Would you like some fruit?   How much traffic is there on the road?

I have some interesting information.   There was so much work to do.

Can you give me some information?

2 We often use *a* or the plural when referring to things in **general** and *the* when referring to things in **particular**:

I wish I had a banana.   = there are many bananas and I wish I had one of them

I've got a car.   = there are many cars and I've got one

The banana I had was nasty but the orange was nice.

      = the particular banana and orange that I ate

I need to take the car to the garage.   = my car in particular

I love bananas and oranges.   = in general

New cars are better than old ones.   = in general

3 We use *a* or *an* before names of **professions**, but not before **subjects** studied:

I want to be a doctor.   That's why I'm studying medicine.

4 We leave out *the* or *a* in some prepositional phrases:

You should go to bed.   He's at work.

but not in other prepositional phrases:

He sat down in **the** middle of the road.   She was in **a** terrible muddle.

5 Most **place names** do not have *the* at the beginning:

Britain   Cambridge   Cairo   Oxford Street   etc.

BUT some do:

the USA   the Netherlands   the UK   the Atlantic   the Alps   etc.

4 Past simple and present perfect

1 We use the **past simple** to talk about what happened at a particular time in the past:

The Second World War started in 1939.

My sister got married last year.

I saw a film about animals on TV last Wednesday evening.

In 2002 I spent my summer holidays in America.

When did you go to New York?

2 We use the **present perfect** to talk about what happened in the past:

a When no definite time in the past is given or known:

Have you ever visited Paris?   I have been to Greece several times.

He has seen that film before.

b When the activity began in the past and has not yet finished, or is still relevant:

I have (already) read 100 pages of the book.   No food for me, thanks – I've already eaten.

c When the activity finished recently:

I have (just) been to the dentist's.   I have finished my work at last.

3 The **present perfect** is often used with these adverbs:

just   already   before   never   yet   so far   ever

Have you done your homework yet?   I have never seen a lion in the wild.

She hasn't visited the UK before.   Have you ever driven a BMW?

4 The **present perfect** is *not* used to talk about a **definite time** in the past and is *not* used in questions that begin: *When . . . ?*

And we always use the **past simple** with phrases like these:

last month   in July   on Wednesday   yesterday   a few minutes ago

✓ I saw that film last week.   ✗ I have seen that film last week.

✓ We did this exercise on Monday.   ✗ We have done this exercise on Monday.

✓ When did you go there?   ✗ When have you gone there?

5 Modal verbs – 1

see also 21: Modal verbs – 2

1   *Can* is used to talk about **ability**:

   Alex can't swim.   Tony can speak Spanish very well.
   I can't find my pen anywhere.   Can you drive a car?

2   *Could* and *will* are used to make **requests**:

   Could you open the door, please?   Please will you open the door?

3   *May, can* and *could* are used to ask for and give **permission**:

   May I open the door, please?   Could I open the door, please?
   Can I leave early today?   You can open the window if you like.

4   *Can, can't* and *mustn't* are used to talk about what is **permitted** and not permitted (forbidden):

   You can borrow books from a library.
   You can't borrow books from a bookshop.
   You mustn't/can't write in a library book.   = You aren't **allowed** to write in a library book.

5   *Must, need to* and *have to* are used to talk about **obligation** and lack of obligation:

   You must use a pen to fill in this form.   = You have to use a pen to fill in this form.
   You don't have to write in capitals.   = You needn't write in capitals.

   Need to is used in positive statements, but *need not* (no *to*) is used in negative statements:

   You need to get up now.
   You needn't do your homework until tomorrow.

6   *Should* is used when giving or asking for **advice**:

   You should write clearly.   = I advise you to write clearly.
   You shouldn't forget to read the instructions.   = Don't forget to read them.
   Should I write to him or phone him?   = Do you advise me to write or phone?

7   *May* and *might* are used when talking about **possibility**:

   It might rain tomorrow.   = It is possible that it will rain.
   The sun may come out soon.   = It is possible that the sun will come out.

6 The future

1   We use *will* to make **predictions** and **general statements** about the future:

   I expect it will be sunny tomorrow.   This time tomorrow I'll be on the plane to London.
   I'll be thinking about you while you're on the plane.
   This time next year we'll be in our new flat – if everything goes according to plan.

2   We don't normally use *will* or *'ll* in a clause following a **time conjunction**:

   when   if   until   before   after   while   by the time
   If you are free tomorrow, will you be able to help me?
   I'll finish preparing the meal before our guests arrive.

3   We normally only use the short form *'ll* after **pronouns**:

   I'll see you tomorrow.   It'll be sunny tomorrow.

   but in writing, or for emphasis, we often use the full form *will* (sometimes underlined):

   I <u>will</u> see you tomorrow – definitely!   It will be sunny tomorrow.

   We use the **present continuous** (or *going to*) for **arrangements**:

   I'm meeting them at 7.30.   We're visiting Spain next year.
   I'm going to meet them at 7.30.   I'm seeing the dentist this afternoon.

   We use the **present simple** to talk about **fixed events** on a timetable or calendar:

   The exam takes place on June 13th and 14th.   (= it's in the calendar)
   Our flight takes off at 17:30.   (= it's in the timetable)

   We use *going to* for **inevitable** future events that are sure to happen:

   His wife's going to have a baby.   Quick! The train is going to leave any minute!

We use *going to* to talk about **intentions**:

I'm going to catch the 9 o'clock train.   We're going to visit my grandparents this weekend.

I'm not going to do my homework until I have more time.

4 We use *will* to make **promises**, **suggestions** and **offers**:

I'll help you if you like.   I'll do the cooking if you do the washing-up later.

I won't help you unless you ask me.   I won't forget to phone her.

Shall is used when making a suggestion:

✓ Shall we meet for a coffee this evening?   ✗ Will we meet for a coffee this evening?

7 *Wh–* questions

1 *Yes/No* questions usually end with a **rising tone**:

Does he live in London? ↗   — Yes, he does.

Are you feeling all right? ↗   — Yes, thanks.

Have you ever visited the United States? ↗   — No, I haven't.

Did you remember to phone home last night? ↗   — Oh no, I didn't.

Is Toronto the capital of Canada? ↗   — I don't think so.

2 *Wh–* questions ask for specific information, and can't be answered with *Yes* or *No*:

What   *What . . . for*   *When*   *Where*   *Which*   *Who*   *Why*

How   *How many*   *How much*

What did you see yesterday?   Who did you give that book to?

What did you do that for?   Why have you brought an umbrella?

Where did you put my keys?   How did you manage to solve the problem?

Which drink will you choose?   How many cakes have you eaten?

Wh– questions usually end with a **falling tone**:

Who are you writing to? ↘   — I'm writing to my aunt.

Where does she live? ↘   — In Canada, in Ottawa in fact.

When did you see her last? ↘   — A long time ago – I was about ten I think.

Why don't you see her more often? ↘   — It's a long way to Canada.

3 *Who . . .*, *What . . .* or *Which . . .* can also be the subject of the sentence:

What surprised you most about the film?   — The ending.

Which town sounded more interesting?   — The first one.

✓ Who wrote to you?   ✗ Who did write to you?

4 It is sometimes more polite to use an **indirect question** rather than a direct question:

How old are you?   →   May I ask how old you are?

Where's the toilet?   →   Do you know where the toilet is?

What did you do last night?   →   Can you tell me what you did last night?

Where do you live?   →   ✓ Could you tell me where you live?

    ✗ Could you tell me where do you live?

8 Reported speech

see also 13: Reported questions

1 In reported speech the tense usually changes 'one step back' to the **past** or to the **past perfect**:

'I haven't been to Poland.'   →   He said that he hadn't been to Poland.

'I don't often read the newspaper.'   →   She said that she didn't often read the newspaper.

'I'll phone you when I get home.'   →   He said that he would phone me when he got home.

'Why are you looking so surprised?'   →   She asked me why I was looking so surprised.

But if the information is still **relevant** or **true**, the tense needn't be changed:

My boss refused to let me know whether I'm going to get a pay rise next year.

We were told that Jupiter is the largest planet.

2 Reported **statements** are introduced by verbs like these, followed by *that*:

add admit announce answer complain explain find out inform someone let someone know reply report say shout suggest tell someone whisper etc.

'I'm afraid I made a mistake.'	→	She admitted that she had made a mistake.
'Oh, and I'm sorry.'	→	She added that she was sorry.
'Listen everyone: we're getting married!'	→	They announced that they were getting married.

3 Statements made **recently** are normally reported with **present tense** verbs:

'I'm feeling sick.'	→	He says that he's feeling sick.
'It's too difficult.'	→	He thinks that it's too difficult.

4 Reported **orders**, **promises**, **offers**, **requests** and **advice** are introduced by verbs like these, followed by *to . . .*:

advise ask encourage invite offer order persuade promise recommend remind tell threaten want warn

'You'd better be careful.'	→	She advised me to be careful.
'Will you help me, please?'	→	He asked me to help him.
'Don't drop it.'	→	She warned me not to drop it.

9 and 23 *–ing* and *to . . .*

1 *–ing* is used as the **subject** of a sentence:

Preparing a meal every day is hard work.   Eating out every day is expensive.
Living abroad is interesting.   Washing up after a meal isn't much fun.

2 *–ing* is used after **prepositions**:

Is anyone interested in joining me for a drink?   I'm looking forward to going away on holiday.
I can't get used to drinking tea without sugar.   I was very tired after running to catch the bus.

3 Most **adjectives** are followed by *to . . .* (the infinitive):

pleased glad surprised disappointed relieved shocked interesting kind hard difficult easy etc.

I was pleased to receive your invitation.   It was kind of you to invite me.
We were surprised to get a bill for £45.   It was easier to do than I had expected.
We were sorry to hear your bad news.   He was afraid to open the door.

BUT some adjectives are followed by a **preposition** + *–ing* (see **2** above). For example:

afraid of interested in sorry about good at capable of famous for fond of etc.

She's afraid of flying.   He's fond of collecting butterflies.
We're sorry about interrupting.   They're very good at ski-ing.

4 *to . . .* is also used in the structures: *too . . . to . . .* and *. . . enough to . . .*:

We arrived early enough to get a seat.   This coffee is too hot to drink.
The tray was too heavy for me to carry.   Boiled eggs are easy enough to cook.

5 Some **verbs** are usually followed by *–ing*:

avoid can't help delay dislike don't mind enjoy finish give up practise etc.

I've finished preparing the salad.   I'm trying to give up smoking.
I avoid staying in expensive hotels.   I dislike doing the washing-up after a meal.
I couldn't help laughing when he fell over.   I always enjoy trying new dishes.

6 Some **verbs** are usually followed by *to . . .*:

afford agree choose decide expect forget hope learn manage mean need offer pretend promise refuse try want would like allow someone encourage someone force someone help someone persuade someone teach someone etc.

I'd like you to help me to do the washing-up.   She persuaded me to help her.
They promised to invite me to lunch.   He didn't mean to spill the soup.
I can't afford to stay at the Ritz.   We decided to have a drink in the pub.
We managed to get a table by the window.   He tried to open the jar.

7 Some **verbs** are followed by *–ing* or by *to . . .* with **no** difference in meaning:

begin continue intend hate like love prefer propose start etc.

She began to eat/eating her meal.   I love to eat/eating Chinese food.
I don't like eating/to eat alone in restaurants.   Which dessert do you intend to order/ordering?
After the meal we continued chatting/to chat for a long time.

10 Comparing

1 If an adjective has one syllable the comparative ends in *–er*, and single consonants are doubled:
> *fresh · fresher   simple · simpler   big · bigger   fat · fatter*

If an adjective ends in *–y* the comparative ends in *–ier*:
> *tasty · tastier   easy · easier   healthy · healthier*

If it has two or more syllables, the comparative form normally uses *more*:
> *more important   more expensive   more difficult*

Remember these irregular comparatives:
> *good/well · better   bad/badly · worse*

2 We can use *like* or *the same as* to talk about similarities:
> Mineral water often tastes like tap water.
> Mineral water often tastes the same as tap water.

3 We use *as . . . as* to talk about differences as well as similarities:
> An apple is just as tasty as a banana.
> Fruit is not as sweet as chocolate.

4 We can compare things by using *more . . . than* or *–er than*:
> Champagne is more expensive than wine.
> Wine is cheaper than champagne.

Or we can use *not as . . . as* or *less . . . than*:
> Champagne is not as fizzy as Coke.
> Champagne is less fizzy than Coke.

Or we can use *as much . . . as* or *as many . . . as*:
> There is not as much fat in margarine as in butter.
> There are not as many calories in low-fat milk as in full-fat milk.

5 We can use *enough . . . to* to mean 'as much as necessary':
> We don't have enough time to cook a meal tonight.
> Do you have enough cash to pay the bill?

We can use *too . . . to* to mean 'more than we like or want':
> This ice cream is too cold for me to eat yet.
> There are too many dishes on the menu to choose from/to know what to order!

11 The passive

1 The passive is used when the person responsible for an action is **not known** or **not important**:
> Glass is made from sand.
> Scissors are used for cutting paper.
> I was given a watch for my birthday.
> The results will be published on Monday.

Or when we want to **avoid** mentioning the person responsible for an action:
> You were asked to arrive at 8 a.m. (less 'personal' than: 'I asked you to arrive')
> This composition must be handed in by next Monday.

2 *By* is often used with the passive to emphasize **who** was responsible for an action:
> Penicillin was discovered by Alexander Fleming.
> The first CDs were marketed in 1982 by Philips and Sony.
> The research is being done by a team of European scientists.

3 Often there's no great difference in meaning between a passive and an active sentence. The passive can be used to give variety to the **style** of a passage, as in these examples:
> Only 17 muscles are used when you smile but 43 are used when you frown.
>   You only use 17 muscles when you smile but you use 43 when you frown.
> Light bulbs were invented in 1879 by Joseph Swan.
>   Joseph Swan invented the light bulb in 1879.

4 Using the passive tends to make a sentence sound **more formal** and **less personal** than an active sentence, as in these examples:

> The battery pack and charger are included in the price.
> We include the battery pack and charger in the price.
> Your money will be refunded in full if you are not totally satisfied.
> We will refund your money in full if you are not totally satisfied.

12 and 17 *If . . .* sentences

1 We use *If . . .* + **present**, followed by *will*, to talk about the probable **consequences** of events that are **likely** to happen, or to describe the consequences of events that **always** or **usually** happen:

> If our flight lands on time, **we**'ll arrive in time for lunch.
> If you book your summer holiday in December, **you**'ll get a discount.
> If you intend to go to the USA, **you**'ll have to get a visa.
> If I'm feeling ill tomorrow, I'll stay at home.
> If water is heated to 100°C it will boil.

2 We use *If . . .* + **past**, followed by *would*, to imagine the possible **consequences** of events that are **unlikely** to happen or events that **can't possibly** happen:

> What would you do if you could go anywhere in the world?
> — If I had enough money, I'd go to Brazil.
> If you had £1,000, where would you spend your holiday?
> If I was (or were) English, I wouldn't need to go to English lessons.

3 We often use *If I were you . . .* , followed by *would*, when **giving advice**:

> If I were you, I wouldn't go home yet.
> If I were you, I'd stay at home.

4 We use *If . . .* + **past perfect**, followed by *would have* + **past participle**, when we want to imagine the possible **consequences** of events that happened (or didn't happen) **in the past**:

> If there hadn't been a mix-up with our booking, we'd have had a room with a view.
> If I had known about the delay, I wouldn't have got to the airport so early.
> If you had reminded me to confirm the booking, I'd have written a letter.
> If you had arrived earlier, we would have got a table overlooking the sea.

5 *Unless* means *if not* :

> I can't do it if you don't help me. = I can't do it unless you help me.

Even if is a stronger form of *if*:

> Even if you pay me a million pounds, I won't do it.

13 Reported questions

see also 8: Reported speech

1 Reported questions are introduced by **verbs** like these:

> *didn't know   asked   inquired   tried to find out   wondered   wanted to know*
> 'What's the time?'   ➡   She wanted to know what the time was.
> 'When did you arrive?'   ➡   He wondered when I had arrived.

2 Questions are reported with a **change in word-order** from direct speech:

> 'Is this true?'   ➡   He asked me if it was true.
> 'When is it going to happen?'   ➡   He wanted to know when it was going to happen.

3 *Yes/No* questions are reported with *if* or *whether* :

> 'Is it Tuesday?'   ➡   He asked me if/whether it was Tuesday.
> 'Are you feeling all right?'   ➡   She asked me if/whether I was feeling all right.

4 Questions asked **recently** are normally reported with **present tense** verbs:

> 'Are you OK?'   ➡   He wants to know if you're OK.
> 'Why is it so difficult for you?' ➡   He wonders why it's so difficult.

14 Past simple and past continuous

1 We mostly use the **past simple** to talk about events that happened in the past:

    I went home at 6 o'clock.   I didn't get up till lunchtime.

2 We use the **past continuous** to talk about activities that were **interrupted** or had **not finished** at the time mentioned:

    At 7.45 last night it was still raining.   It was raining when we arrived but now it has stopped.
    I was having a lovely dream when the alarm clock went off.

or to refer to **simultaneous** events or activities:

    What were you doing while I was waiting for you?

15 Past perfect

1 The **past perfect** is normally used to **emphasize** that one past event happened **before** another:

    Before we got our cat, we had never had a pet in our family.
    I hadn't realized he was married until I noticed his wedding ring.
    I had been feeling quite depressed until my friend called round to cheer me up.

It's not necessary to use the **past perfect** when events are listed in the order they happened:

    He left the house, unlocked his car and drove off.
    I saw his wedding ring and realized he was married.

2 The **past perfect** is very common in **reported speech**:

'I went there last year.'	→	He said that he had been there the previous year.
'I've been there once.'	→	She said that she had been there once.
'I paid you the money yesterday.'	→	I told you that I'd paid you the money the day before.

16 see 3: Articles and quantifiers
17 see 12: *If . . .* **sentences**

18 *For* and *since*

1 We use the **present perfect simple** to talk about activities which have **finished** happening, but are **still relevant** now:

    I have been to Italy several times.   He has seen that film three times.

We often use the **present perfect simple** when talking about numbers or quantities:

    I have read 100 pages of the book.   We have reached page 55 in our book.

2 We use the **present perfect continuous** to **emphasize** that an activity is **still** going on. We often use it with *for* or *since*:

    I have been playing football since I was seven.   = I still play
    The children have been playing in the garden since seven o'clock.   = they are still playing
    What have you been doing today?
    – I've been lying in bed, reading a book.

Notice the difference between these examples:

    Someone has eaten my chocolate.   = all my chocolate
    Someone has been eating my chocolate.   = some of my chocolate
    I've been reading *War and Peace*.   = I am still reading it
    I've read *War and Peace*.   = I have read the whole book!

3 *for* is used with a **period** of time:

    ✓ for two years   for a long time   for a few minutes   for the last three days
    ✗ since two years   ✗ since a long time etc.

since is used with a **point** in time:

    since 1988   since yesterday   since 5 o'clock   since lunchtime   since April

Grammar reference

19 Relative clauses

1 **Identifying** relative clauses identify **which** person or thing we are talking about. We use *who, that, which, where* or *whose* to form identifying relative clauses, with no commas:

> One of his sons is a doctor, one is a dentist. The son who is a doctor lives in London. The son who is a dentist lives in Bristol.
>
> He is the man who I told you about.   = He is the man that I told you about.
>
> This is the thing which you need.   = This is the thing that you need.
>
> She's the girl whose father won the prize.

> (*Who* and *whose* only refer to people, *that* and *which* refer to things or people.)

2 If *who, that* or *which* is the **object** of an identifying relative clause it can be left out:

> He is the man I told you about.
>
> This is the thing you need.

3 **Non-identifying** relative clauses contain **extra** information, sometimes added as an afterthought. We use *who, which, where, when* or *whose* to form non-identifying relative clauses. Notice the use of **commas** in the examples:

> My mother, who is 67, likes sweets.
>
> My house, which is 100 years old, is falling to pieces.
>
> The winter of 1812, when Napoleon went to Russia, was very cold.

4 Non-identifying relative clauses can also be used to **join** sentences, and are more common in writing than in conversation:

> She is very shy, which I find surprising.
>
> I'm in love with Chris, who is a wonderful person.

20 Conjunctions

1 We can join two short sentences to make a longer one by using these conjunctions:

Time   *and*   *and then*   *before*   *after*   *while*   *as*   *during the time*

> He opened the envelope and took out the letter.
>
> He put on his glasses before he read the letter.   or   . . . before reading the letter.
>
> He smiled to himself as/while he read the letter.   or   . . . while reading the letter.

Reason, cause or consequence   *and*   *because*   *so*   *so . . . that*   *such a . . . that* etc.

> I wanted to read the book because my friend had recommended it.
>
> It was a delicious cake and I ate it very quickly.
>
> My friend said it was a good book, so I decided to read it.
>
> The book was so exciting that I couldn't put it down.
>
> It was such a good book that I stayed up all night reading it.

Contrast   *but*   *although*   *even though*

> Even though I tried very hard, I didn't manage to finish the book.
>
> It was a good book, but I couldn't finish it.

2 To show **purpose**, we can use *to . . . /in order to/so as to . . .* or *so that*:

> I used a dictionary to/in order to/so as to look up any unfamiliar words.
>
> I took some books with me so that I would have something to do on my holiday.

21 Modal verbs – 2

see also 5: Modal verbs – 1

1 *Could* and *was/were able to* are used to talk about past **ability**:

> Alex couldn't swim very well, but Tony could swim like a fish.
>
> I couldn't find my pen anywhere.
>
> I couldn't have done it without your help.
>
> She was able to finish her work.
>
>   BUT: She could finish her work.   = It is possible she can finish (now or soon).
>
> Were you able to mend the washing machine?
>
>   BUT: Could you mend the washing machine?   = Please mend it (now or soon).

2 *Must have* and *can't have* are used to talk about past **probability**:

    She must have got lost.   = She has probably got lost.

    She can't have finished yet.   = She has probably not finished.

3 *Might have* and *could have* are used to talk about past **possibility**:

    She might have got lost.   = She has possibly got lost.

    He might have been joking.

    You could have found it if you'd looked harder.

4 *Have to* is used to talk about past **obligation** and lack of obligation:

    I had to use a pen to fill in this form.

    I didn't have to write in capitals.   = it wasn't necessary to

5 *Should have* is used to **criticize** someone or **regret** something:

    You should have filled in the form more clearly.   = You did the wrong thing.

    You shouldn't have forgotten to read the instructions.

    I should have phoned you to tell you the party was cancelled.

---

22 Prepositions – 2

1 Some verbs are often followed by a **preposition**:

blame someone for   concentrate on   congratulate someone on   forgive someone for   look at   look for praise someone for   prepare for   punish someone for   remind someone of   thank someone for walk past   etc.

    I looked at the instructions but I couldn't understand them.

    I'm looking for my keys, but I can't find them.

    They praised him for his performance.

    We thanked her for the present she gave us.

2 Some verbs + preposition have an **idiomatic** meaning and it's hard to guess their meanings from their parts:

    do without   get over   look after   make for   see through   see to   etc.

    I can't do without a cup of coffee in the morning.   = manage without having

    She was very upset, but she soon got over it.   = recovered

    Please look after my cat while I'm away.   = take care of

3 Notice the correct and incorrect **word order** in these examples:

    ✓ He jumped off the cliff.   ✓ He jumped off it.

    ✗ He jumped the cliff off.   ✗ He jumped it off.

---

23 see 9:–*ing* and *to* . . .

---

24 Two-word verbs

1 Many two-word verbs (**phrasal verbs**) have **literal meanings**. We can combine verbs of motion with adverbs to make lots of different two-word verbs:

verb	*bring*	*climb*	*come*	*drive*	*jump*	*march*	*pull*	*push*	*run*	etc.
+ adverb	*away*	*back*	*down*	*in*	*off*	*on*	*out*	*over*	*past*	*up*	etc.

    The general saluted as the soldiers marched past.

    Please go away and don't come back.

    He walked away without a word, slamming the door as he went out.

    The train was already moving when he jumped on.

    ✓ She drove away with my coat in the car.   ✗ She drove with my coat in the car away.

2 A **transitive** two-word verb (verb + adverb) is followed by a noun or pronoun:

    do up   find out   give away   give back   look up   make up   put on   see off   etc.

    I'll come to the station to see you off.

    I can find out the information on the Internet.

    ✓ I looked up a word.   ✓ I looked a word up.   ✓ I looked it up.   ✗ I looked up it.

    ✓ I put on my coat.   ✓ I put my coat on.   ✓ I put it on.   ✗ I put on it.

3 Some phrasal verbs are formed from *be* + adverb:

It's time for me to be off. I'll be over to see you tomorrow.

I'll be along later.

4 An intransitive two-word verb (verb + adverb) is **not** followed by a noun or pronoun:

fall over   get out   get up   give up   look out   run away   etc.

Look out, there's a car coming! She was running so fast that she fell over.

5 Some two-word verbs are followed by a preposition:

look forward to   look out for   look up to   make off with   make up for   run away with   run out of   etc.

Look out for the rocks when you swim out.

She ran away with her husband's brother.

✓ I look up to my aunt. ✗ I look my aunt up to. = I admire and respect her

✓ I look up to her. ✗ I look her up to.

25 Adverbs and word order

1 Some adverbs are normally placed in mid-position in a sentence, between the subject and the verb:

almost   always   certainly   completely   ever   frequently   hardly   hardly ever   just   nearly   never   obviously   often   probably   rarely   seldom   etc.

I always make notes before writing. I hardly ever eat shellfish.

I never watch TV in the daytime. He probably likes seafood.

If a sentence contains a modal verb or auxiliary verb, these adverbs fit after it and before the main verb:

✓ He will certainly be arrested. ✗ He will be certainly arrested.

✓ He can never be arrested. ✗ He can be never arrested.

✓ I can never eat oysters. ✗ I can eat oysters never.

✓ I have just eaten a lovely lobster. ✗ I just have eaten a lobster.

2 Other adverbs may fit 'more comfortably' at the end of a sentence, or the end of a clause:

yesterday   today   last week   in the afternoon   one day   etc.

happily   heartily   loudly   well   badly   etc.

We went to the zoo yesterday. We're going to the beach tomorrow.

He plays the trumpet loudly and badly. She was smiling happily.

3 Some adverbs can go at the beginning, in the middle or at the end:

soon   recently   unexpectedly   quickly   slowly   suddenly   etc.

Soon you'll be happy. You'll soon be happy. You'll be happy soon.

Suddenly he started laughing. He suddenly started laughing. He started laughing suddenly.

4 An adverb doesn't normally fit between a verb and a direct object:

✓ I like tennis very much. ✗ I like very much tennis.

✓ He drove the car very fast. ✗ He drove very fast the car.

✓ He plays basketball badly. ✗ He badly plays basketball.

Communication activities

1

1 Read what the colours say about you:

BLACK	You are intelligent and serious.
BLUE	You like fresh air and being outdoors, and you like cold weather.
BROWN	You like to be in charge and tell others what to do.
GREEN	You care about the environment and love animals.
PINK	You laugh a lot and don't take things too seriously.
PURPLE	You like to be alone and 'do your own thing'.
RED	You have strong feelings and a quick temper.
WHITE	You like things to be tidy and clean, and you always plan ahead.
YELLOW	You are a happy, friendly person, and you love being in the sun.
GREY	You are ambitious and work hard.

2 👥 Discuss which parts of this interpretation of your personalities are right, and which parts are wrong.

2

Here are some ideas to help you to remember things. Suggest these ideas to your partners and find out their reactions.

To remember phone numbers:
- repeat the number out loud several times
- break the number down into parts to remember it better

To remember people's names:
- think of one special characteristic of that person
- think of the place where you first met

To remember new words:
- highlight the words with a coloured pen
- write the words again and again

To remember things you have to do:
- make a To Do list every day
- set the alarm on your watch or mobile phone to remind you

3

Find out from your partner who these people are, and add them to the family tree:

Quentin   Ursula   Victor   Nora   Zoë   Yasmin

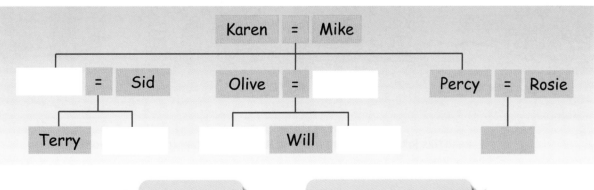

Who is Karen?
Who is Quentin?

— Karen? She's Mike's wife.

4

Tell your partner about these places in London:

Millennium Bridge 2001	architect Norman Foster, sculptor Anthony Caro	footbridge linking St Paul's on North Bank with Tate Modern and Shakespeare's Globe Theatre on South Bank
St Paul's Cathedral 17th century	rebuilt by Sir Christopher Wren after the Great Fire of London in 1666	Whispering Gallery – a whisper at one side carries all round the dome Stone Gallery – great view of the city
Tate Modern 1998	former electric power station, now an art museum	20th and 21st century art in an enormous building; admission free

5

Tell your partner the story of this film:

Jonathan and Sara are complete strangers. They meet in a New York department store while Christmas shopping, have a wonderful afternoon together and have hot chocolate at a famous café called Serendipity and wonder if fate will bring them together again. Sara comes up with a way to test fate and see if they are truly meant to be together. Jonathan writes his name on a $5 bill, which she spends. She writes her name inside a book and sells it to a second-hand book stall.

Some years later they are both engaged (to other people). Jon asks his best friend (and soon-to-be best man) to help him find Sara's book and Sara. They start at the store where Jon and Sara first met.

Meanwhile, before Sara's own wedding, she flies from California to New York with her best friend. Jon and Sara keep going to the same places, but just miss being there at the same time. In the end, of course, they do meet at the same café. And the story ends happily.

6

Look at the picture story and spend a few moments thinking about what you can say about it. Then tell your story to your partner. You start.

7

Read this joke through and then tell it to your partner in your own words:

A man goes into a cinema with his dog to watch a film. It's a romantic comedy and when there's a funny scene the dog starts laughing. A little later on there's a sad part and suddenly the dog starts crying.

This goes on throughout the entire film, with the dog laughing and crying at all the right places. A man sitting a few rows back has witnessed the entire thing and decides to follow the man out. Outside the cinema, he approaches the dog owner and says, 'That's truly amazing!'

'It certainly is,' the dog owner replies, 'He hated the book!'

8 How to make yogurt

Boil milk for one minute.

Leave milk to cool to body temperature.

Mix in some yogurt to act as a starter.

Pour into a jar and cover loosely.

Put in a warm place until morning.

The next morning, you'll have yogurt!

Put it in the refrigerator to chill.

Serve with honey, nuts, or fruit. Enjoy!

9 Ask your partner to talk about these topics. Use follow-up questions to encourage him or her to tell you more:

- Do you like zoos?
- Is it OK to hunt birds and wild animals?
- Would you like to have a garden and grow plants and flowers in it?

1 You begin, by asking the first question.

10 Explain this problem to your partner and ask for advice on what to do:

'I have a terribly stiff neck. It gets worse the longer I sit down, but I have to do a lot of studying so I spend a lot of time sitting down. What can I do?'

2 Your partner will ask you for advice. These exercises may help – explain them to your partner.

Start with both feet flat on the floor.

1   Raise your right heel as high as you can. Hold for three seconds.
2   Lower your heel to the floor, and raise your toes off the ground. Hold for three seconds.
3   Lift your foot and straighten your leg. Hold for three seconds.
4   Point your foot down, clench your toes together, keeping your leg straight. Hold for three seconds.

Do the same with your left foot. Repeat the exercise five times for each foot.

11

In both parts of this role play your name is **SANDY**. Read these instructions carefully before you begin the phone calls.

Don't look at each other during the calls. Pretend that you are really on the phone.

First call   First make this call to your partner:

> It's 2 o'clock. You're on a train on your way to meet your friend Billy, but the train is late. Call Billy and if he isn't there, leave him this message:
> 'My train is running late. I will be late for our meeting this afternoon. I'll meet him at 4 o'clock instead of 3.30. I'll ring if there are any more delays. Billy can call me on my mobile: 0707 128923.'
> Check that the message has been taken correctly. Say thank you and goodbye.

Second call   Now Terry will call you on the phone:

> It's 3 o'clock. You are still on the train, which is going to be even later than you expected. You are just about to call Billy again, when your mobile rings . . .

12

The people you recognize in the pictures are shown in green.

Adam wears glasses.   **Ellen** plays tennis.
Charlie is wearing a baseball cap.   **Gina** has long hair.

Find out about the ones you don't recognize by asking your partner questions:

> *What's the name of the one who has curly hair?*
> *— That's Bill.*
> *Oh, Bill, yes. He's the one who was in my brother's class at school.*

David has just lost his job.   **Hazel** is giving a concert tonight.
Bill was in my brother's class at school.   **Fanny** was my sister's best friend at school.

13

Your friend's **Uncle Joe** was late for work each day last week. Your partner knows the reasons but can you guess why? Use the phrases on the right as you make your guesses.

Your partner will try to guess why your **Aunt Doris** was late for work. Here are the reasons:

Monday	the trains were on strike
Tuesday	she overslept
Wednesday	she missed the train
Thursday	she got on the wrong train
Friday	she took the day off

> He   might have . . .
>   can't have . . .
>   must have . . .
>   could have . . .
>   shouldn't have . . .
>   should have . . .

14

Ask your partner these questions. Use the phrases on page 63 to encourage your partner to explain more.

* Do you like hot weather? Cold weather?
* Would you like to live in a wetter country? Or a drier country?
* Is the weather getting better every year?

You begin, by asking the first question.

15

Read this story and then tell it to your partner in your own words:

ATM Gives Out Free Cash

An ATM machine at Ramsey National Bank went mad in Fargo, North Dakota last Monday. It gave out free cash, but three honest bank customers ignored temptation and returned the free money.

'All I wanted was $20 to go to the movie,' said Mary Davidson. 'Then $20 bills just started shooting out of the machine.' In total, the machine gave out $125 to Davidson.

Barb Hofland's first attempt to withdraw $100 from the money machine failed. On her second try, she got her $100 – and another $100. 'I thought I might go shopping, but I just couldn't. It wasn't my money,' she said.

A third customer returned another $60 cash to the bank.

'It was like being in Las Vegas without all the lights and noise,' said Marietta Rasmussen, a Ramsey National Bank supervisor. 'The bank would have lost only $285. But this proves that North Dakota is rich in honesty. I'm glad we're in North Dakota,' she said. 'Somebody out East or West may not have had our same values.'

The cold weather had caused the ATM cash door to stick, so some customers who wanted to withdraw money could not get it. The door opened for other customers, who then ended up with their own cash as well as the cash belonging to the previous customers.

Rasmussen said the machine has now been fixed.

16

Take turns to describe each person in this picture to your partner. Start with the first woman on the top left and continue clockwise.

17

Here are the answers

(The match.)

(She woke up the man who was snoring in the next room.)

(The hairdresser with the terrible haircut cuts the other one's hair.)

(So his salon, though dirty, is the place to go to for a good haircut.)

(I went to bed before sunset and the blinds were open.)

18

Your partner has the sharp version of the blurred picture on the right.

19

Rehearse these jokes and then perform them for the other pair:

Doctor, doctor, I think I'm a dog.
— How long have you felt like this?
Ever since I was a puppy!

Doctor, doctor, I think I need glasses.
— You certainly do, this is a bank!

Doctor, doctor I keep thinking there is two of me.
— One at a time please.

Doctor, doctor, I think I'm a dog!
— Sit!

Doctor, doctor, my sister thinks she is a lift!
— Well, tell her to come in.
I can't, she doesn't stop at this floor!

20

Check your answers:

appóintment dóctor exám examinátion
gymnástics hóspital informátion médicine
operátion pólitics proféssor pronunciátion
qualificátions témperature tréatment

21

 Read what your picture says about your personality:

If your house is made up of clear, thick lines, you are a strong leader.
If your house is made up of wavy, thin lines, you are often indecisive.

If your door is detailed, your life is orderly and predictable.
If your door has no details, your life is often full of changes.

If you drew only one window, you are shy and reserved.
If you drew more than one window, you are talkative and sociable.

If your bedroom is on the ground floor, you plan things carefully.
If your bedroom is on the top floor, you take risks.

If you added a flower to your garden, you are looking for love.
If you added an animal in your garden, you are generous.

2 👥 Discuss which parts of this interpretation are right – and which are wrong.

22

Here are some ideas for helping you to remember things. Suggest these ideas to your partners and find out their reactions:

To remember phone numbers:
- write them down immediately

To remember people's names:
- try to remember the first letter of their name
- say their name out loud when you first meet them

To remember new words:
- look them up in a dictionary and read the example sentences
- keep a vocabulary notebook with a new page for each topic
- write a sentence using the new words

To remember things you have to do:
- keep a diary
- make notes on your mobile phone

23

Find out from your partner who these people are, and add them to the family tree:

Karen   Olive   Rosie   Terry   Will

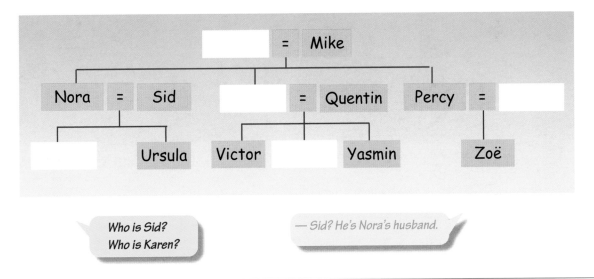

Who is Sid?
Who is Karen?

— Sid? He's Nora's husband.

24

Tell your partner about these places in London:

Tower Bridge 1894	London's most famous bridge	150,000 vehicles cross it every day. Over 900 times a year the roadway lifts to let tall ships and cruise liners pass through. You can visit the original Victorian engine rooms. And from the high-level walkways you can look out across the modern city skyline.
Tower of London 11th century	historic castle, prison and palace	See the Crown Jewels. Experience the history of London. Built by William the Conqueror soon after 1066.

25

Tell your partner the story of this film:

Rob Gordon is mad about pop music and making lists. He owns a record store in Chicago. Dick and Barry work for him there. Dick is polite and shy, and lonely. Barry is loud and tactless, and he enjoys being rude to the customers.

But they are all quite miserable and we wonder: Are they listening to pop music because they are miserable? Or are they miserable because they listen to pop music?

When Rob's girlfriend, Laura, leaves him, he makes a list of his previous girlfriends, and why he broke up with them. He contacts each of them and meets them again. But each meeting is a disaster.

Meanwhile Laura has started dating Rob's dreadful neighbour, Ian. Rob is very jealous. Laura's father dies and Rob goes to the funeral. After this he and Laura get back together again. Dick has a girlfriend and Barry turns out to be a great singer.

26

Look at the picture story and spend a few moments thinking about what you can say about it. First listen to your partner's story. Then tell your story to your partner.

27

1 👥 **Compare your scores:**

21 or more	Wow, you are a sporty person! How do you have time for anything else?
11–20	You are certainly a sports fan, but there seem to be other things in your life.
5–10	You take an interest in sports but you have plenty of other interests too.
4 or less	OK, so sports are not your thing. Never mind, some people just don't like sports.

2 👥 **Categorize the sports in the list on page 68 under the following headings:**

outdoor sports
popular spectator sports
all-year-round sports
not really sports at all?

solo sports
competitive sports
indoor sports

summer-only sports
team sports
ball games

28

Ask your partner to talk about these topics. Use follow-up questions to encourage him or her to tell you more:

- Is it OK to keep a dog in a city apartment?
- Do you like animals?
- Would you like to live in the country?

Your partner will begin by asking you a question.

Communication activities

29   How to repair a scratched CD

Find a CD that always skips while playing.

Hold the CD up to a bright light.

Look for scratch on the bottom side of the CD.

Put a small amount of toothpaste on a cloth.

Place CD onto a flat, clean surface.

Polish the CD until the scratch disappears.

Clean with water and dry completely.

Insert CD into player, and enjoy the music!

30

1   **Your partner will ask you for advice. These exercises may help – explain them to your partner.**

 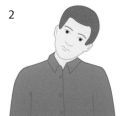 

1   Slowly lean your head to the right. Rest it gently in this position for three seconds as you breathe out.

2   Repeat to the left. Do the exercise on each side three times.

3   Bend your head slowly forward and back three times. Don't move your head quickly. Don't move your head round and round.

2   **Explain this problem to your partner and ask for advice on what to do:**

'My legs ache when I sit at my desk for long periods. What can I do?'

31

In both parts of this role play your name is TERRY. Read these instructions carefully before you begin the phone calls.

Don't look at each other during the calls. Pretend that you are really on the phone.

First call   First your partner will call you on the phone:

It's 2 o'clock. Your flat-mate, Billy, has just gone out. Offer to take a message. Write down any important information.

Second call   Now make this call to your partner (Sandy):

It's 3 o'clock. Call Sandy on the phone:
Billy still hasn't returned. He has probably gone directly to the meeting point. He hasn't got his mobile with him. You couldn't give him the message.

32

The people you recognize in the pictures are shown in green:

Bill has curly hair.
David rides a motor bike.

Fanny is a flight attendant.
Hazel plays the violin.

Find out about the ones you don't recognize by asking your partner questions:

> *What's the name of the one who's wearing glasses?*
> — *That's Adam.*
> *Oh, Adam, yes. He's the one who I met in London.*

I met **Adam** in London.
Charlie used to work with my father.

Ellen went to school with me.
Gina was my first teacher.

33

Discuss these questions:

- What did you see on the left of the picture?
- What did you see on the right of the picture?
- What did you see at the top of the picture?
- Did you notice what was visible in the distance?
- How many buses did you notice?
- How many motorbikes did you see?
- Did you notice which way the traffic was heading?
- Did you see how pedestrians were able to cross the road?

34

Your friend's **Aunt Doris** was late for work each day last week. Your partner knows the reasons why but can you guess? Use the phrases on the right as you make your guesses.

Your partner will try to guess why your **Uncle Joe** was late for work. Here are the reasons:

Monday	his alarm clock didn't go off
Tuesday	it was raining hard
Wednesday	there was a traffic hold-up
Thursday	someone stole his bike
Friday	he wasn't feeling well

> *She might have . . .*
> *can't have . . .*
> *must have . . .*
> *could have . . .*
> *shouldn't have . . .*
> *should have . . .*

35

Read this story and then tell it to your partner in your own words:

Police Use Special Cars to Catch Car Thieves

Police in the Arizona area have arrested at least six people since they began using special bait cars to attract would-be car thieves.

Police officers park the cars in areas that have the highest number of thefts, usually shopping centers or apartment complexes. Each vehicle has a camera, a microphone and sensors that set off an alarm at the police control centre.

If a thief opens the door or starts one of the cars, the control center calls in the closest patrol officers. Meanwhile a computer screen shows the vehicle's location and speed every eight seconds with the help of a global positioning system device in the car.

'The response time is very quick, within one or two minutes,' said auto theft expert Sgt. Dave Mauser.

When officers get close enough, the control center activates a remote switch that kills the engine. Police rush in as the car coasts to a stop. The suspects usually can't escape because the system locks the passengers inside.

Each police department has its own special vehicles, donated by insurance companies.

36

Take turns to describe each person in this picture to your partner. Start with the first man in the back row and continue clockwise.

37

Check your answers. The corrections are underlined in green.

A 'Series Of Unfortunate Events' aren't like normal books. The children's misfortune begins when their parents are killed when their house is burnt down. Even though they have a lot of bad luck, I thought the books were amazing. I am on the third one now and all of them so far have been really excellent. It's a real page-turner, 'The Bad Beginning', and its sequel. I would recommend these books to anyone of any age. It didn't matter to me that there was no happy ending, it's really the story that counts and how the author writes it.

I am a child and thought that all you bookworms out there would like to read a review from a young person's point of view. This enchanting book was so good I literally couldn't put it down. Lemony Snicket can make you laugh and cry at the same time. 'The Bad Beginning' is about three little children: Violet (the oldest), then Klaus and baby Sunny. They soon unfortunately find out from one of their parents' closest friends that their beloved mother and father have died in a fire in their own home. They are sent to live with a long-lost relative called Count Olaf. Even from his name you can guess that he is most probably is very unkind and frightening. The three orphans still have lots of misfortune to come in this book and the rest of the series to come. I definitely advise you to read this book if you want to be in a dreamland of imagination.

38

Your partner has the sharp version of the blurred picture on the right:

39

Read this joke through and then tell it to your partner in your own words:

A police officer sees a man driving around with a pickup truck full of penguins. He pulls the man over and says: 'You can't drive around with penguins in this town! Take them to the zoo immediately.'

The man says OK, and drives away.

The next day, the officer sees the man driving around with the truck still full of penguins, and they're all wearing sunglasses. He pulls the man over and demands: 'I thought I told you to take these penguins to the zoo yesterday.'

The man replies: 'I did . . . today I'm taking them to the beach!'

40

Ask your partner these questions. Use the phrases on page 63 to encourage your partner to explain more.

- Do you like rainy weather?
- Would you like to live in a hotter country? Or a colder country?
- Do you think the climate is changing?
- Does the weather affect your behaviour?

Your partner will begin by asking you a question.

41

Rehearse these jokes and then perform them for the other pair:

Doctor, doctor, I've lost my memory!
— When did this happen?
When did what happen?

Doctor, doctor, I think I'm a telephone.
— Well, take these pills and if they don't work then give me a ring!

Doctor, doctor, I snore so loudly I keep myself awake.
— Sleep in another room then!

Doctor, doctor, my son has swallowed my pen, what should I do?
— Use a pencil till I get there.

Doctor, doctor, everyone keeps ignoring me.
— Next please!

42

👥 Look at this picture for **TWO** minutes only, and talk about what you can see:

Now look at Activity 33 on page 140.

43

Check your answers:

walking	seat	beat	hat	match	Jan
working	sit	bit	hut	much	John
	set	bet	heart	march	Jean
	sat	bat			June

44

Check your answers:

Jánuary Fébruary Ápril Julý Augúst Septémber Octóber Novémber

45

Check your answers:

	5 chair	9 share	13 mouth
2 really	6 rarely	10 Mary	14 now
3 like	7 lake	11 fear	15 fair or fare
4 hate	8 height	12 hall	16 hole or whole

Map of the book

	Topic vocabulary development	Grammar practice	Vocabulary	Pronunciation
1 Personal information	personalities + colours	Present simple and past simple		Numbers
2 Learning English	language + communication	Prepositions – 1	Using a dictionary	
3 Money	shopping	Articles and quantifiers – 1		Vowels – 1
4 Education	teaching + learning	Past simple and present perfect	Collocations – 1	
5 Relationships	relatives	Modal verbs – 1	*Un*–, *in*– and *im*–	
6 Travel and holidays	holidays	The future		Vowels – 2: diphthongs
7 Where I live	homes + apartments	*Wh*– questions		Intonation – 1
8 Entertainment	films	Reported speech	Opposites	
9 Communication	feelings + emotions	*–ing* and *to* . . . – 1	Collocations – 2	
10 Food and drink	eating, drinking + cooking	Comparing		Consonants
11 Science and technology	tools + gadgets	The passive	Suffixes – 1	
12 Around the world	place names + geography	*If* . . . sentences – 1	Nationalities and adjectives	
13 Weather and climate	weather	Reported questions	Suffixes – 2: nouns	
14 Nature	animals, plants + the environment	Past simple and past continuous	Abbreviations and symbols, etc.	
15 Free time	hobbies + sports	Past perfect	'False friends'	
16 Good health	health + parts of the body	Articles and quantifiers – 2		Stressing the correct syllable
17 Puzzles and problems		*If* . . . sentences – 2	*Make*, *take* and *do*	
18 The future	plans + possibilities	*For* and *since*	UK and USA English	
19 Work	jobs + professions	Relative clauses	Words with similar meanings	
20 Transport	traffic and travel	Conjunctions	Looking, seeing, watching	Recognizing tones of voice
21 The past	history	Modal verbs – 2		
22 The news	news	Prepositions – 2	Spelling and pronunciation	
23 Books	reading for pleasure	*–ing* and *to* . . . – 2	Two-word words	
24 People	friends	Two-word verbs	Two-word verbs	
25 That's funny!	humour	Adverbs and word order		Reading aloud